The 8th Madness

An Anthology

Compiled by

Dominic Ward

For

Dirt Heart Pharmacy Press

2015

'The 8th Madness'

'An Anthology; complied by Dominic Ward

For Dirt Heart Pharmacy Press'

30th September 2015

Esk, Queensland

978-0-9944167-1-1

Cover by Brion Poloncic

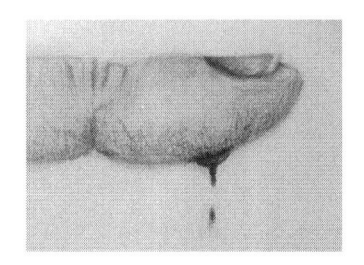

Norman Conquest

Derek Pell

Jason E. Rolfe

Eckhard Gerdes

Jønathan Lyons

Brion Poloncic

Carolyn Chun

Peter Hobson

Carla M. Wilson

Tom Griffin

Ben Pullar

Harry McCullagh

Not Dead but Dreaming

Jason E. Rolfe

From his small corner office, Daniil Ivanovich Yuvachev often spent his lunch hour staring out the window. He imagined walking along Bolshaya Konushennaya Ulitsa, or down Nevsky Prospekt toward the Moyka River where, depending on the day, he could envision either the sun rippling off the water's surface, or his body floating face down beneath the Zelyony Bridge.

Daniil Ivanovich's mind frequently wandered up and down Nevsky Prospekt, habitually stopping at St. Petersburg's most renowned book store. The House of Books occupied one of the loveliest buildings on Nevsky Prospekt – the Singer Company Building, an innovative and richly decorated Art Nouveau masterpiece. It stood near the intersection of Nevsky Prospekt and the Griboedov Canal, opposite Kazan Cathedral. Despite passing both the House of Books and Kazan Cathedral twice daily on his way to and from work, Daniil Ivanovich had never actually set foot inside either building – at least not in any real sense. During its meanderings, his mind once visited the cathedral, and it almost always stopped at the House of Books. His mind admired the building's elegance, from its large ground floor windows to its graceful glass-roofed atrium. Its wrought bronze sculptures, weathered green by time and Russian weather, blended beautifully with the reddish-grey granite façade. The interior, Daniil Ivanovich heard, had recently been restored, yet his mind still envisioned the time-worn Art Nouveau walls and ceilings he had seen in old photographs. While Daniil sat alone in the small corner office overlooking the union of Bolshaya Konushennaya Ulitsa and Nevsky Prospekt, his mind explored the House of Books, imagining the works of writers such as Daniil Kharms and Mikhail Zoshchenko, both of whom worked, once upon a time, within the walls of the Singer Company Building (while it still housed the Leningrad Children's State Publisher).

The hour allotted for his lunch never left Daniil Ivanovich's mind with enough time to fully explore the book store, let alone the Arts Square or the Russian Museum (a mere stone's throw away from the Singer

Company Building). If, after all, his mind wandered too far from his office, it would not have a chance to get back, and his boss always scheduled his meetings right after lunch. It was, Daniil Ivanovich noted, the Old Man's way of ensuring that his workers returned promptly. Those who arrived late were escorted from the building as a reminder to those who showed up in a regulated manner.

Daniil Ivanovich's primary role with The Company involved the writing, filing, and shredding of reports. He was greeted each and every morning by the same list of forty-two required reports. He spent the first three hours of his day writing them, the next three filing them. Between the fourth and fifth hours he took a brief lunch and, as previously discussed, stared out the office window while his mind wandered along Nevsky Prospekt. When his mind returned from its brief jaunts, Daniil Ivanovich attended the Old Man's meeting. The reports were never discussed. The Old Man preached the need for a passionate, enthusiastic workforce willing to surrender its life to The Company and its glorious ideals. He said these things in such a way that each and every employee understood them as unquestionable commands rather than encouraging prosaicisms. After the meeting, Daniil Ivanovich finished filing the forty-two reports, and then spent the final three hours of his day shredding them (for reasons known only to the Old Man).

One Wednesday afternoon, Daniil Ivanovich's mind, having wandered down Nevsky Prospekt to The House of Books, sat savoring a copy of Aleksei Remizov's *The Clock*, when it caught the emerald green eyes of a young woman who, it so happened, held a copy of the same Remizov's *The Fifth Pestilence*.

"Have you read Remizov before?" she asked.

"I imagine I have," Daniil Ivanovich's mind replied. "You?"

"I haven't," the young woman said. "Would you recommend him?"

"I would! Are you a fan of fantastic literature?"

The young woman frowned and shook her head. "Not particularly, but I'd love to learn more about it. Would you care for conversation and a cup of coffee?"

"I've read that the coffee here is terrible," Daniil Ivanovich's itinerant mind replied.

"Ah, but I have it on very good authority that the conversation is excellent!"

Daniil Ivanovich's mind remembered the Old Man's meeting. He knew that if he stayed for coffee he would likely be late. "I can't," he replied. "I must get back to work. The Old Man is a stickler for timeliness."

"Surely a few minutes wouldn't kill you!"

"I can't say that for certain," Daniil Ivanovich's mind replied. It pictured the Old Man's unpleasant, slightly sinister smile, and the tears of those dismissed from his employ never to be seen again. "Can we meet tomorrow?"

The young woman with the emerald green eyes shrugged and smiled. "Maybe. Come back tomorrow. If I'm here we can chat about fantastic and bizarre literature."

Daniil Ivanovich's mind raced back up Nevsky Prospekt. Its return coincided with a knock on his office door.

"The Old Man's meeting!" Alexander Stepanovich grinned. "You don't want to be late!"

###

That evening, while Daniil Ivanovich walked from his place of employment to the Nevsky Prospekt metro station, he thought about the young woman his roving mind had met earlier that day. It dawned on him that he had not gotten her name.

"I forgot to ask!" his mind cried out.

"What an idiot!" Daniil Ivanovich yelled. His voice startled the commuters standing near him. They eyed him warily.

His mind, weary of waiting for the metro and aware that its fellow commuters were annoyed by Daniil Ivanovich's behavior, ambled home on its own. It thought about dinner and the book it hoped to finish before bed (Nikolai Leskov's *The Enchanted Wanderer*). Mostly, though, it thought about the young woman with the emerald green eyes. By the time Daniil Ivanovich reached home, the dinner his mind cooked up had failed due to the lack of requisite ingredients and he was forced to eat canned soup with stale saltines. His copy of *The Enchanted Wanderer* was no more than an old essay written in a crumbling newspaper his father had once used to wrap a delicate picture frame. After dinner, Daniil Ivanovich lay down in bed. He closed his eyes and his mind pieced together a tale that only slightly resembled the one actually penned by Leskov.

###

When Daniil Ivanovich Yuvachev left for work the next morning his destination was, as always, the five story office building adjacent to the Mertens Trade House on Nevsky Prospekt. It was the only building on Nevsky Prospekt that Daniil Ivanovich knew with any certainty. In fact, it could be argued that the small five story office building adjacent to the Mertens Trade House on Nevsky Prospekt was the only building, outside his small apartment, the neighborhood grocery story, and a few insignificant little shops that Daniil Ivanovich had ever actually visited. Work ate away the hours, washing them down with a heavy mixture of energy and motivation, leaving him with little more than a strong desire for sleep. The daily writing, filing, and shredding of reports, it could be said, had an extremely soporific effect on him.

Throughout the morning Daniil Ivanovich wrote the requisite reports, forty-two in total. Shortly after he had finished filling in the final details he began filing the freshly minted pages alphabetically by last name. By the time he had reached Krestovsky it was time for lunch.

He left the filing room and returned to his office where, with a giddy sort of nervousness, he sat down at his desk and looked out the window at Nevsky Prospekt. The street was perpetually busy. He imagined brushing past noonday shoppers, lunch-bound businessmen, and literary tourists. He saw beggars and children and imagined the early winter chill. With a slight shiver, his mind wandered down Nevsky Prospekt toward the House of Books. It noticed a sign on the glass door – back in fifteen minutes – and cursed. If it waited the full fifteen minutes, Daniil Ivanovich's mind would never make it back in time for the Old Man's meeting. It glanced around, hoping it might spy the young woman with the emerald green eyes. The bustling shoppers and drab workers ignored him as each, lost in their own thoughts, made their way to or from the places that mattered only to them.

Daniil Ivanovich's mind waited ten minutes, but the House of Books remained closed and the young woman never appeared. The disconsolate mind made its way back up Nevsky Prospekt to the five story office building adjacent to the Mertens Trade House. It was greeted by the voice of Daniil Ivanovich's friend and fellow worker, Fyodor Mikhailovich.

"The Old Man's meeting," said Fyodor Mikhailovich (who was at times an idiot, but that is neither here nor there). "Don't be late!"

Following the meeting Daniil Ivanovich finished filing his reports alphabetically by last name. Once Zoshchenko's file had found its place, he returned to Akhmatova and began meticulously shredding each new report. Daniil Ivanovich had spent ten years with The Company, and for ten years he had spent each afternoon (save for Sundays) shredding the same reports he had spent every morning (save for Sundays) writing. Once Zoshchenko's report disappeared, Daniil Ivanovich returned to his office. He reclaimed his hat and coat and walked the short distance between his office building and the Nevsky Prospekt metro station, his mind still lost in the young woman's eyes.

###

Since his mind's first meeting with the young woman, Daniil Ivanovich had found it increasingly difficult to keep the thing from wandering. When he reached the five story office building adjacent to the Mertens Trade House earlier this morning, for example, his mind continued drifting down Nevsky Prospekt toward the still-closed House of Books. It was the fact (and only the fact) that the book store would not open for another three hours that convinced his mind to follow him up five flights of stairs to his small corner office, and it was with great reluctance that his mind prepared to write the first of his forty-two reports. While it is true that the writing of these reports did not require Daniil Ivanovich's mind, he felt much more comfortable knowing it was safe within his head rather than wandering the streets of St. Petersburg unsupervised. That aside, he was still afraid his mind would wander too far and for too long, and that he would miss the Old Man's meeting. He could not afford time, books, three square meals or higher education on his current salary, nor could he afford to lose that salary. Such was the shackling of his life and soul to the dull-grey cinderblock of labor.

If asked, Daniil Ivanovich Yuvachev would have said that today was like any other day he had spent working for The Company. Everything felt perfectly ordinary. That is to say, nothing felt remotely extraordinary at all, until Daniil Ivanovich turned his attention to the list of reports the Old Man required him to write, file, and later that same day shred. There were forty-three names on the list. One more than the previous day, and the day before that, and each and every day before that dating back ten years. Daniil Ivanovich studied the list. He knew the names by heart, from Akhmatova to Zoshchenko and back again. While an official photograph accompanied each name, they were names and nothing more. In fact, the longer he worked for The Company, the less name-like the names became. They soon became mere words, and after that nothing more than their corresponding numbers. Akhmatova, for example, was one. Zoshchenko was forty-two. He was always forty-two. For the past decade, Zoshchenko had been his forty-second report each and every day. The forty-second report written, the forty-second report filed, and ultimately the forty-second report shredded at day's end. Today, however, Zoshchenko would be the forty-third report Daniil Ivanovich wrote, filed, and eventually destroyed. The list contained a new name and, with it, a new photograph. Her photograph. The young woman with the emerald green eyes looked up at him from the folder on his small metal desk. "Esther," he said. "Her name is Esther." For the first time in a very long time, Daniil Ivanovich thought about work. He read Esther's report closely, and in doing so learned a little bit about her. For example, green-eyed Esther attended the state university in St. Petersburg. The state university in St. Petersburg was one of Russia's most prominent schools, or so Daniil Ivanovich (who lacked higher education, or the time required to do anything more than read about such places in the newspaper) understood. It was the school of writers such as Chernyshevsky and Turgenev, of poets such as Blok and Brodsky, of communist revolutionary politicians and political theorists who served as leader of the Russian Soviet Federative Socialist Republic from 1917 and of the Soviet Union from 1922 until their death such as Vladimir Lenin. Esther, unlike Lenin, belonged to the Institute of Philosophy, an institute known for its high standards of education in the fields of philosophy, ethics, cultural, religious and conflict studies.

It was, Daniil Ivanovich noted, understandable then that Esther, a studious philosopher, should take a professional interest in his wandering mind. While he hoped that more basic desires would eventually overtake Esther's desire for knowledge, he knew that without a body to basically desire she had very little to go on. "Perhaps my mind can somehow convince her to meet the rest of me for dinner tonight," he mused.

Daniil Ivanovich tried returning his attention to the remaining reports, but his mind refused to relinquish focus. "In ten years you've never questioned these reports," it told him. "We don't know a thing about them – what they mean, why we write, file, and shred them every day."

"Do you remember Pasha?"

"Of course I remember Pasha," Daniil Ivanovich's mind replied. "This used to be his job."

"Until he questioned the purpose of these reports," Daniil Ivanovich said. "He was dismissed after that, and hasn't been seen since, I might add."

"I know you better than you know yourself," his mind said. "You've never even considered questioning the Old Man's need for these reports. But now," it added, with a touch of mischievousness, "Now you're curious."

It was true. Esther's appearance on the Old Man's list sparked Daniil Ivanovich's imagination – something ten years of work had numbed into irrelevance. "Maybe," he whispered.

"Maybe it's time you found out what these reports are really all about."

###

Daniil Ivanovich went to see Nikolai Vasilievich. His friend and fellow worker was on his way to lunch. The two men were soon joined by those who also wrote, filed, and destroyed reports on a daily basis. These men shared the same hour for lunch. "Why do we write these reports?" Daniil Ivanovich asked. "Why bother filing them if they are to be shredded by the end of the day?"

Several colleagues shushed him with a ferocity Daniil Ivanovich found alarming.

"What purpose do these reports actually serve?" he asked.

Nikolai Vasilievich glared at him. The others looked around uneasily, his question an obvious source of fear and consternation. "Be quiet," Nikolai Vasilievich warned him.

"You don't know either," Daniil Ivanovich said. "None of you do. We write these same reports each and every morning only to shred them in the afternoon. Who reads them? Does anyone read them? Does anybody care about what we do, day-in-day out, each and every single day of our lives (except Sundays)?"

"We work," Nikolai Vasilievich replied. "That's what we do, Daniil Ivanovich. We work day–in, day-out, each and every single day of our lives (except Sundays). Isn't that enough for you?"

"Work is a fine thing," Daniil Ivanovich replied. "But what does it mean?"

"It means shelter," Nikolai Vasilievich said. "It means food on our plates and shirts on our back."

"But," Daniil Ivanovich asked, "Is that all it means? What about the names, the people, who are they?"

"What names? What people?"

"On the reports," Daniil Ivanovich insisted. "The Old Man added a name to my list this morning. I'd like to know why?"

"But why do you want to know why?" Nikolai Vasilievich demanded. "My father wrote, filed, and destroyed reports for The Company day-in, day-out, each and every single day of his life (except Sundays), as did his father before him. They never knew why, never wondered, never asked, they just did."

"There must be a reason. I want to know, need to know, that what I do matters, that it means something."

Nikolai Vasilievich laughed. "Nothing we do, at work or play, means anything at all, Daniil Ivanovich. You're searching for meaning where no meaning exists. Now be quiet before the Old Man hears you."

###

Daniil Ivanovich returned to his office. He sat down behind his small metal desk, turned his chair toward the window and the world beyond its dusty glass, and closed his eyes. His impatient mind all but leapt along Nevsky Prospekt toward the House of Books.

Esther welcomed it with a warm smile. She carried with her Remizov's *On a Field Azure* and the Strugatsky brothers' *Definitely Maybe*. "If I didn't know better," she said, "I'd think you came here looking for me."

"I confess," Daniil Ivanovich's mind said. "I did miss you yesterday. The store was closed when I wandered by."

"Do you wander often?"

"Every day."

"Perhaps you'd like to wander over to the café for a cup of coffee? We can discuss the fantastic and bizarre to our hearts' content."

"I'd love to!"

As they made their way toward the café, Daniil Ivanovich Yuvachev's mind said something it felt with every inch and ounce of its being. "This means something."

###

Daniil Ivanovich's mind wandered farther down Nevsky Prospekt than it should have, smitten as it was by the lovely young woman. It sat listening to her talk. It explored the sparkling emerald of her eyes while envisioning future dates and dinners and hours spent strolling along Nevsky Prospekt together. In short, it completely lost track of the time.

At precisely one o'clock, Nikolai Vasilievich, who often wrote about St. Petersburg, knocked on Daniil Ivanovich's office door and said, "Time for the Old Man's meeting. You don't want to be late!"

When his friend and fellow worker failed to respond, Nikolai Vasilievich knocked again and said, "Daniil Ivanovich, the Old Man's meeting. Let's go!" Daniil Ivanovich Yuvachev, however, remained seated, staring silently out his office window. Nikolai Vasilievich waved his hand in front of his colleague's smiling face. He stepped around the small metal desk and stood between Daniil Ivanovich and Nevsky Prospekt, but his friend's gaze remained vacant. To Nikolai Vasilievich, the younger man's eyes were like windows opening onto an empty room.

"Is he dead?" Alexander Stepanovich asked, peering over Nikolai's shoulder.

"No, not dead" Nikolai Vasilievich mused. "Not anymore. Now he's dreaming."

Jacaranda Blues

Harry McCullagh

Despite the fans whirring noisily in its corners, the air inside St Joseph's Catholic Church was stifling and my comfort wasn't improved by the dark charcoal suit I had chosen to wear. It was quite unsuitable for the weather but I wanted to wear something dark to the funeral of my best friend, Mary Bryan. A chubby young priest with a catholic name, either Damien or Donovan, I wasn't paying that much attention, spoke soothing words about Mary and her achievements. I was pretty sure he had never met her but he outlined her life in a kind of shorthand everyone could understand. When the young priest mentioned Mary's name for the first time, a pigeon flew through the open doors and straight into the stained glass windows behind him. A gasp rose from the congregation as the bird fell lifeless to the floor.

It had only been four day since Mary died and I still felt numb. Looking at the lifeless bird, it's pathetically small thin frame and wings bent at impossible angles, reminded me of Mary and I broke down. At first soundlessly sobbing then as tears ran in rivulets down my face, in a noisy raking anguish. I buried my face in my hands and tried to compose myself before I stood to speak about Mary, her life, her work and her mysteries. I hoped beyond desperation that I could be dried eyed and matter of fact when my part in her brilliant life's final pageant was played out. While the priest talked I watched a storm slowly ride the horizon towards us, it's distant thunder rumbling like muffled drums. It would be raining by the time we got to the grave side. "Norwegian Wood" by the Beatles, one of Mary's favourite songs, was played and suddenly it my turn to speak.

Five hours later, standing in my kitchen surrounded by friends and family of the departed, I was coerced into reciting the poetry of the woman we had just buried. I knew it by heart. It was our story. As I stood there loudly declaiming the songs of childhood's end from over twenty years before, I suffered my first heart attack.

That I survived, surprised even me and I made a number of changes to my life which brings me here, exactly a year later. Except for the heat of October, the tropical storms that could be relied on almost every afternoon and the blooming of the Jacarandas so much had changed. I had quit my job, gone freelance and had made all those life altering changes we normally wait too long to do. The calendar on the wall told me that it was the first anniversary of Mary's death. In four days it would be a year since we buried her and since I almost joined her. At first I had floated not really knowing what to do. Then six months ago I heard rumours that plans were being made somewhere deep within that cesspool that is London's literary circle of ex-pats, for a biography of Mary Bryan. I couldn't imagine anything worse than some hack armed with 100 duty free camel, a small expense account and access to as much Kinko's photocopying as he needed, searching the net for juicy titbits and parlaying Mary's writing into a tatty adventure yarn for the young leftists, pseudo feminists and the boring underfed romantic undergrads who still admired her poetry and her lifestyle.

So that is how I came to be sitting here, in the converted bedroom of a worker's cottage in Auchenflower writing the biography of my best friend. What really spurred it was the report in the Courier Mail of Mary's death. An article and two photographs. The first was of a tall thin but obviously female body leaning against the sturdy trunk of a Moreton Bay Fig. I had taken the photograph sometime in the early nineteen eighties in the old Brisbane botanical gardens and have never found out how the press obtained it. Then there was the black banner headline screaming "Poet dead at 49" . It wasn't even right. She was only 47. Under it was another photo. This one had been taken with a long range lens and showed Mary's corpse under a blanket on a gurney as it was being pushed towards an ambulance. A shock of dark curly hair fell sideways from out under the blanket. A horrid little detail captured forever. If you look closely you can see me standing in the corner, a garden gnome, watching, stock still. That was the first time that my heart could truly be said to have missed a beat. The two photos could scarcely be more different. One, though ancient now, oozed life and promise and the other, so much later spoke of death. I noticed a trembling in my hand and that tremor became my focus as the words blurred. The tremor told me I was alive. I bit my bottom lip till it bled and dropped my black eyes back to the paper.

I put the clipping back down on my work table. Placing it gently between a number of other clippings and photographs devoted to Mary. It had taken me six months to start to accept her loss. Accept it and deal with it but I still was not coping with it.

I am unable to remember which stories are true and which are false, especially the earlier ones which we had invented to give us a cache, a past, a story or some infamy. That we later tried to live those lies is part of the story. I am the only one left of our circle who knows how to lie so convincingly that it will be taken as the truth and to tell the truth so inexpertly that it will be taken as a lie thus I am well placed to record that which history should know and that which should be left to sleep with the dead.

Lives are not just events that can be recorded but are also our dreams and nightmares. It is what makes me the most apt chronicler of her life. Well that and the fact that I kept everything. Well in truth. at first, my mother did. She kept the letters and postcards that came to her from Mary and I while we explored the world. Hastily written notes on the back of cheap Nepalese postcards assuring loved ones that we were okay. Long letters written in style of literary masters describing views and items of interest. Hand drawn pencils sketches of the pyramids, of the Eiffel tower and the Tower of London. Photos of Mary naked, swimming in the North Sea, the Baltic, the cobbled coastal beaches of England and the sands of Greece.

We wrote of our youth in large letters and many colours and looking back they are like a child's drawing stuck to the door of the Fridge. But it is what wasn't said that is of most importance. The letters don't tell of cold nights on Eurail, cuddling up to keep warm, or to keep one's pocket from being picked, of the predators that waited at the major train stations looking for the lost or the weak or the just plain lonely or the million other small travails that one puts up with when young. They don't tell of the fights and the divergence of character, the shattering of bonds thought unbreakable, or the tears and anger of betrayal. They told facts and dreams but not nightmares to family and friends who might have wondered what had become to 'those two.'

Ours was a friendship that lasted over thirty years. The early days were easiest when friendship came to us as a natural gift and we delighted in each other's company so much so we preferred it to the company of others. In High School people thought we were a couple but in truth we weren't. I had known her eight years before I kissed her and even then it was on a dare. It was our last day of school and she asked me if I was still going to be the only boy in our form year who hadn't kissed her. So I did. I grabbed her and kissed her hard on the lips and felt her tongue find mine. My hand crept snakelike around her waist and I felt for the first time in passion, the rise and fall of her breasts against me.

School had passed in a blur. We were part of a blue grey herd that was being corralled down a learning path that had been set for us and suddenly we were at University. Mary did journalism, I did economics arguing it was better way to understand the capitalist power broking elite only to be reminded by Mary that I was predestined (or was in pre-ordained) "to become a dull provincial accountant working for the public service". A prophesy fulfilled. I ceased work after her funeral after 25 years as a Government Accountant.

While I mastered accrual accounting and the drinking cheap red wine in student union soirées in the refect, Mary fucked anything that moved and in a rather reflective and nostalgia driven letter written to me from London shortly after the first diagnosis "several things that didn't." Despite myself I laughed at the image this conveyed. It was so very Mary. Whenever I questioned her about her activities she would calm me by saying she may have fucked others but with me she made love. It would calm me only so long as I didn't think too much about it.

That letter outlined what she had been doing the last few years. These were the years I didn't know. Her incredible journey through war zones, parties and politics. It was also the letter that first told me of her illness. It had been a long rambling letter of over twenty handwritten pages littered with joy filled nostalgic references and on the last page there was a signature, huge, scrawled and covering a quarter of the page. There was no "yours faithfully" or even "yours" but an "I love you" written in a different coloured pen. Green. So very Mary, using green or purple just to irk me, knowing those colours were used only for audit. A thumbing of a nose to the accountant I had become. Underneath it all was a Postscript written in purple and in a hand far shakier than the rest. "I'm thinking of coming home"

It made me think of that day back in 1981 when I told Mary that I was going home. Europe was something I had to do before I went home to grow up but for Mary it was much more. Europe would be her finishing school or rather a blank canvas upon which her life could be painted. There was something big happening in Europe at that time. Change danced all about us and Berlin was swinging again, safe in a reputation of artistic freedom and gothic sex fostered by people like Bowie and Iggy Pop. We watched arty films and saw grim cabarets and immersed ourselves in European culture.

It was in this environment of studied decadence that Mary sold her first article to Associated Press. When it was published in America in Time it caused a sensation. By sheer luck, talent or opportunism Mary had visited Gdansk for some poetry reading sponsored by the Polish government and had spoken to the men who would soon start shaking the east to its knees, the workers of the Gdansk shipyards. Her article broke the story of the major discontent in Poland. It made her and as a result Mary worked more at her craft while I skulked around the cold wet streets. I had run out of money, but Mary's writing had bought us a suite in one of Berlin's better hotels. It was paid for with 'American money' which she spent like water, as if it had no value at all. We talked less and less and then one morning she flew to London without telling me she was going and though she returned that same day it was like some bond between us had broken. Later she informed me that "Jacaranda Blues", a volume of poetry written on the road, was to be published. These were poems to me, about me, about us. They were my life and hers, combined, distilled and mixed. I was jealous, angry, betrayed and felt a little left behind. My emotions built a wall up between us and I later thought it was somewhat ironic that it had happened in Berlin. We were standing next to the wall and I found myself looking south west towards the Tempelhof airport, towards my future and when I looked back I noticed that Mary was looking east. All it took were some sad lonely words and a quick almost embarrassing embrace and she was gone and so was I.

I heard no more till Jack was born. Jack is our son. That day we parted by the wall I did not know he had been conceived and I have always wondered whether Mary knew. These were the things that the biography can never show. No one knows. In our last days, despite the tension, we still made love at every opportunity. I still woke to poems and verses left around the room. Scraps and snippets of poems, funny observations "Your underwear has found religion - it's holey" and practical advices such as "buy milk." When I received, by parcel post, several months later, a printer's proof copy of Jacaranda Blues, I recognised many of the poems. Some had started as scraps left on my pillow when she rose before me. The copy I was sent had a simple dedication "For Tom." printed under the title. The only embellishment added in Mary's hand was a heart with a jagged line going halfway through it. I recognised the symbolism at once. Though our hearts were broken, the connection could never be completely severed.

Jack was born in Berlin at 5.52PM on a Friday. I got the phone call at 5 AM from some German nursing sister to say that a child had been born, a boy, eight pounds, healthy and fair. I went back to bed. Strangely though now we were forever linked I never felt so far removed from Mary as I did then.

After leaving me Mary had found a beautiful blond given to the most outrageous racism called Signe. Of this I can not make too much. Who knows her demons but I always wondered how Mary could have put up with a holocaust denier. Love is strange I guess. Signe was a woman destined to bear the pure Aryan children of the master race who had been born fifty years too late, She was also homosexual and as such would have been one of the regime's victims. When I met her, during one of Mary's rare trips home in those years, Signe and I had argued about the past. I said the Nazi's would have eradicated her for sleeping with women. "Ah" she said" Zen I vould have just fucked men". Just over five years later Mary left her and Signe killed herself after finding that 'just fucking men' could be as hurtful and damaging to one's psyche as one's own sex. She threw herself under a high speed train somewhere between Frankfurt and Berlin.

After returning from Europe, the next twenty years passed for me as they did for
everyone. Slowly at times and then with as speedy rush that one can not imagine. My career prospered from desert boots and cardigan to tailored suits, from working to consulting and finally reaching the pinnacle of 'managing' at the same time as I noticed the hair on my balls growing grey. I soon met and married Margo, a would be socialite, looking for a rising star husband who would broker money and success. We bought the large house in one of the better suburbs with a large mortgage and lived a large life totally beyond our means. Letters would come occasionally from Mary and sometimes from Signe. Mary's were poetic, sad, wistful, fact filled newsletters about anything that caught her fancy. Signe's were simple. They were about Mary, asking questions I never knew the answers to. When the letters arrived Margo would grow silent for days and refer to 'letters from your dyke girlfriend' and the 'mother of your bastard child". At first I

argued but later just retired to my study to read the letters over a glass of scotch. Sometimes I would re-read my favourite poems in Jacaranda Blues. Margo left me when she realised how meagre my ambitions really were. She kept half my house, half my money and both my kids. After Margo, I predicted the trends of the nineties by downsizing myself into the small workers cottage that I bought at auction from the office of the public trustee.

Soon after Signe's suicide, Mary sent Jack back to Australia to live with me. He was about seven then and he did so until Margo and I separated. Unable to cope, I passed Jack on to Mary's mother and set about drinking myself to death. I would have succeeded too but for Mary's intervention. It was 1994 and in that hell called Sarajevo when Mary was blown up when a Jeep she was in hit a land mine. I was contacted by a UN major, a Dutchman called Langbroek, who told me that the body could be collected at the UN compound in Sarajevo and that it was Mary's will that I accompany her remains back to Australia. I booked the next flight out and was somewhere over Saudi when a small mistake was discovered. Mary was not dead. I arrived in Sarajevo having travelled through the siege lines on a journalist passport hastily arranged for me by Mary's employers. I had been drinking since I left Australia and was drunk when I finally stood beside her hospital bed. She opened an eye and looked at me with untold sadness. Her only words "Oh Tom" before she lapsed back into whatever world the drugs had taken her to. Her words were like a slap to my face. Did I appear that ravaged that I could even sadden a dying woman?

As she recovered I begged her to come home with me but she couldn't stop reporting. It had become a drug which carried her along. She was addicted to her life and her quasi celebrity. She had become used to the bullets, burnings, bashings and threats that were daily events of a life lived on the edge. Normal life bored her. Articles under her by-line filled newspapers all around the world. Accolades were laid at her door like garlands before ancient heroes. Now and then a book would appear under her name, back-grounding some war or catastrophe that she had covered. She may have sacrificed sex for love, and career for family but never abandoned an inherent sense of honesty or social justice. There were those who would accuse her of an almost relentless pursuit of fame, or perhaps, infamy and they were wrong. She searched for justice and truth. Fame came with that.

To friends and lovers like me, left treading water in her wake, it took years to work these things out. Our generation paid lip service to glories of difference but still viewed with great suspicion anything or anybody who lived outside of tightly defined view of normal and Mary could be nowhere near 'normal' at times. A complete lack of self preservation meant that, almost always, she could be relied to do the unexpected. This made her great.

It was in August that she called me from Milan asking if now she could come home to die. She wanted to complete the circle. I knew she had cancer but this was the first time she mentioned mortality. In her absence both Brisbane and she had grown but both could still be easily recognised. Though she railed against its innate conservatism she knew it was safe. Others might laugh at Queensland, but after the world, it is the perfect place to lick one's wounds and an almost perfect place to die.

When she arrived home she told me how bad the cancer was. It had started as a particularly virulent form of lung cancer and despite her losing a lung had moved into secondary stages throughout her body. She had smoked unfiltered Camels since she was 19, that she would get cancer was surprising but no surprise. She looked okay when I picked her up at the airport. Just tired but within two weeks she had difficulty walking and within a month of arriving she was bedridden. The end was approaching faster than I knew. Of the end, I have memories of absolute clarity. I recall every detail even the jokes Mary cracked as the cancer ate away at her insides, and as her body was reduced to just skin and bones. Through the pain, She called it "the last daze." I laughed at this dark humour.

Life amazes me. It can withstand the heaviest gale but be blown out by the merest puff of wind. A bullet can stop a heart beat in a mille-second. Hit your head the wrong way and you are dead. A cerebral haemorrhage or heart attack can kill you so quickly that you are dead before you even hit the floor. Cancer, though, is not like that. It eats away at its sufferer like an encroaching tide eroding the shore and with that tide comes the pain.

Towards the end even her sight began to fade. I sat by her bed reading her the newspaper or from books in my library. We played CDs and argued about music. Whether

Nick Cave or Ed Kuepper was better. I supported Ed, after all he was a Brisbane boy like me, though Mary, by virtue of her Berlin years, had become a fan of Cave's. We both agreed on the Go -Betweens, The Saints, Paul Kelly and, of course, her favourites, the Beatles. Mary loved John Lennon's songs. They were like her, sharp, witty and sometimes caustic but always reaching towards humanity. Mornings were filled with words and afternoons with music. Evenings with a sort of silence.

I was reading Voltaire aloud when her beautiful but bony hand grasped at my shirt. I shuddered guiltily because it felt like death was reaching towards me but I leaned in to listen getting so close that I could smell the blood and vomit congealing on her lips and the sour sweat of a body that was literally falling to pieces.

"Tom!" Mary whispered with a sense of urgency then fell back on the bed. Exhausted. I knew what she meant, we had made a pact when she came home. To some that may sound melodramatic. That a person fearing pain may crave death but to Mary it was a heartfelt desire to die on her terms. She had asked me to agree to her plan in words as seductive as any line of love that passed her lips and I had answered without thinking. I agreed and now the time had come.

I cried though I knew it was her choice. With immense effort Mary turned towards me and rested her hand on mine. "I want to die here, in the sun, they…" The voice stopped. The effort of talking was too much. I can still taste the word as I spoke it "okay."

I felt ill and went to the bathroom and locked the door and sat on the commode and wept for us. When she had moved back to Brisbane though she was dying, some part of me dreamed of re-establishing our love. I dreamed of her beating the disease and loving me for being here for her. I dreamed of white haired sex and a life discussing everything and nothing. Now it was evident that these dreams were just a place of refuge and comfort for me as 'the love of my life's' life ebbed away. I was about to lose the biggest thing in my life, and worse I was going to help her die. I did not know if I could do it. It took a while for me to compose myself and return to her bed and when I did, Mary was deathly still. I prayed that death had visited while I was away. I sat next to the bed and looked her and was debating whether to check for vital signs when she stirred. Big wide brown eyes looked up at me and then a raspy whisper. "Tom." I don't know if my name has ever meant so much.

Mary pointed at the dressing table opposite. I looked over and saw it was cluttered with papers and documents. There was a photograph of a partner, long gone and another of a son, rarely seen. There was a dog-eared copy of Joyce's Ulysses and a volume of her masterpiece, the title in purple on the spine, Jacaranda Blues. A combination of images and feelings of Brisbane, our home town mostly written on the road somewhere in Europe. Some of these songs, now studied with all the gravitas academia can muster, were written in 30 seconds with the intention of getting into some Belgian's pants. Poems which describe the shimmering wet tropical heat of a Brisbane afternoon composed whilst we almost froze on a country lane in Scotland.

I got up and walked over and picked it up. "You were lucky with this bullshit hey? Australia's greatest living poet?" Gees, who'd you screw to get that title" A small laugh died on parched lips. "Screw you" Mary whispered but a wavering hand found my arm and squeezed it and then fell asleep again. I got up to get a wet washer to wipe her lips. When I returned she was awake and said one word "now." My tears came again with a rush and she said softly that she loved me in a voice which seemed so much stronger now. Whether it was true or just absolution I don't know but I chose to believe it. She motioned for the book. I handed it over and after what seemed like ages she passed it back to me saying "there, lines 24 to 30." I looked at the open page and started to read. Mary must have seen my lips moving because I heard the words spoke, breathlessly "Aloud".

I read.

"Let me not rot on the ground,
as jacaranda flowers do,
but let me be taken from the tree
while beautiful in bloom"

Now I understood. These words, written all those years ago, were a living will personified. It means nothing that the poem they came from, Jacaranda Blues, was about making love in Europe and remembering home but only that they meant something different now. A plea from a friend to die with dignity. Her dark eyes were closed again and I understood why Mary wanted to die here in my bed. She wanted to die with the smell of a Brisbane afternoon on her nose rather than the sterile smell of antiseptic. I knew she was coming to the end of her journey. Today, maybe tomorrow or at the best the next few days would be the only ones left where she could still make the decision herself. She made it now and I was to help but I didn't know how.

Prior to Mary coming home I had never used a needle. All I could think of was what I had seen in movies. Lonely junkies in dingy surroundings melting tablets in water over a candle. What is enough morphine to kill? I found the morphine sulphate tablets on the dresser where we kept them for use when the pain got too much. I crushed five and then ten with the back of a spoon in a saucer. It didn't look enough so I crushed another five. I pounded the tablets into a fine white powder and then added it to a glass with a small amount of water. It made a paste. I added more and more water and then took a candle not used since the last blackout and lit it. I poured some of the mixture into a tablespoon which I held over the flame. I watched as the mixture liquefied in the spoon, a dark residue forming under the bubbles as the powder burned brown at the bottom of the spoon. When it was clear I took a syringe from the bunch left by the Nurse and carefully drew up as much as I could without drawing up the brown residue. I repeated this till the syringe was full. When the last was drawn up I expelled all the air as I had seen them do on television and turned to see Mary had pulled up her T shirt sleeve. I approached showing her the needle. Despite my best efforts the contents were the dull light brown of rotting jacaranda leaves in the gutter, not clear like I thought. I reached for a swab and Mary laughed. "Do you think I'll get an infection?' Now it was my turn to laugh. I tried to find a vein. My hands were shaking so much and the tears were welling in my eyes that all I saw was a blur.

As I was leaning over, Mary kissed me and guided my hand and the needle towards her arm. She smiled at me and said "thank you." I don't know if I injected her or she did but the drug did enter her vein as I held her and she slipped into euphoria. I put the syringe, candle and spoon back in her drawer. I would get rid of it later. I pushed the chair close to the bed and took her hand in mine then just sat back and waited. Her breathing became shallow, then much softer and then finally just stopped. Her hand, which had been holding mine, never loosened its grip and I had to use my other hand to remove it. I felt for a pulse and couldn't feel one. I kissed her forehead and closed her eyes.

First I rang her doctor. He came around an hour later and signed a death certificate. The primary cause of death, myocardial infarction with the secondary being cancer of the stomach and bowel. The Doctor made no mention of the pinprick in the arm and there would be no autopsy. Death was not unexpected. The cancer was advanced.

I was in a daze now, doing my duty, when I rang our son. This was the phone call I dreaded most. We had been friends before I shipped him to his Grans. After that, hurt, he retreated from us both. He answered on the third ring. "Jack, your mother is dead" I said. There was silence and then I heard those telltale choking sounds of grief. We both put down the phone at the same time.

I made other calls. The funeral directors she had chosen, her friends, my friends and what was left of our families. The house was soon filled with well meaning people hoping to assist me through my grief. I don't know how the press found out but pretty soon the phone was ringing off the hook with phone calls coming from London, Berlin and the USA. I delegated the task of answering the phone to my brother, who merely acted as a secretary saying 'a statement would be issued by the family in the morning'.

Into this madness walked Jack, looking so much like his mother that I thought her ghost had walked into the room. He strode towards me, saying "Where is she? Where is she?" Without a word I grabbed his hand and lead him into the room where Mary's body lay. He grabbed me hard and shook me and then hugged me and we cried together. He was all of her that I had left and I was his only parent now. Mary looked beautiful in death. I asked if he wanted to sit with me while we waited for her body to be taken. He sat in the chair that I had been sitting in for the last month and held the lifeless hand that I had recently put down.

It's funny what we think about at such times. Jack surprised me by asking me what clothes would she be buried in not something deeper. Mary had already arranged that and I pointed to a small bag that she herself had packed shortly after arriving and told him that whatever it was, it was in there. I had never opened it. Jack did. It contained a matching red bra and briefs, a pair of skin-tight Levis, a pair of Dr Martin boots and a 1980's Wham T-shirt that said "CHOOSE LIFE". Despite ourselves we could not help but laugh. It was so her.

That was a year ago. The room in which she died is now my workroom and Jack moved in with me. Occasionally I felt Mary's presence in the house but mainly I just got on with missing her. I was typing the opening paragraph to Mary's biography when Jack called to me. I got up and walked through the house and smiled as I saw him sitting under the jacaranda. With two beers, which he held up. I nodded. A couple of purple flowers had fallen into his hair and at that moment he looked more like his mother that I almost cried. Instead I sat with my son under the tree, and twisted the top off the beer and watched as he pointed to a bird laying against the fence.

"It just sorta flew into it" he said to me "musta broken its neck, poor thing." Then something magical happened, the bird shuddered, flapped its wings and flew back into the air. It soared higher and higher till it was out of my sight. It reminded me of the pigeon which had flown into a window in the church during Mary's funeral service on the first mention of her name only to shake itself back to life and fly out of the church as the coffin was being carried to the hearse. That moment I knew I had both the ending and the title of my book and murmured to myself, the words, "This bird has flown."

models of the solar system

Carolyn Chun

from her cordoned window,

a girl observed in the night sky a lunar eclipse,

a round shadow cast by a round planet.

begin. premise: perfection. to this end symmetry

of form, elegance of rhythm. centrality of perception.

concentric spheres: earth inside the sphere containing

the orbit of the moon, inside the sphere containing

the orbit of Mercury, then Venus, the sun, Mars,

Jupiter, and Saturn, all inside the sphere containing the

fixed stars. beyond the stars heaven, purgatory, hell,

eternity pulled taut in every direction (breathe into it).

what's the expiration date on this? better use up the

ground beef before it goes bad. the Vidalias

in the bottom drawer have begun to rot—why

did we get so many? why did you leave? strange—

again. premise: perfection. to this end alignment

of observation with intuition. Copernicus' heliocentric

model, in which circular orbits are unchanging, moving

forward and backwards in time to encompass eternity with

each gently sweeping revolution of round shouldered planet.

how long can I believe in the perfect circles?

roundfaced moon, center of a Black-Eyed Susan,

zero's empty circle, ripe orange circle—expiring

in the crisper. wasn't infinity better to hold on to?

the circle drawn in the sand? the circular stones

falling from hands? and you, my prodigal circle.

again. premise: perfection. to this end simplicity of

practice. Keppler's elliptical orbits describe the winding

solar system.

but what has been always and will be always are

clear—the fixed orbits, from periapsis to apoapsis,

eyes meeting and then moving away. what has the

ability to hold you except the universe? what is your

trajectory besides momentum? what keeps you

burning—do you know I am sometimes awake all night?

again. premise: perfection. to this end completeness

of thought. Einstein's general relativity bending of

spacetime. the flavor of unification, the taste of food

consumed in a dream. what can we do? how can we

know this is true? the universe, we are told, is

expanding at an increasing rate into dark cold unknown.

that endless night. unquenched drowning in that beautiful
sea.

Or cold

Carolyn Chun

Based on "Abscission," a short film by Bastian Michael

or cold

and alone

or clean

and new

or else

still moving

broken free

creatureless creature

faceless face

nameless also

(who was

he she?)

released wild

again against

naked shoreline

where circling

ripples reach

from that

first dive

or else

in reverse

feet first

dry spring

from out

of the

lake's bullseye

land in

socks shoes

dry rot

ill-fitting business

too tight

around shoulders

too loose

about neck

or the

other way

around perhaps

a word

glimpse or

breeze then

in the

right context

turning time

forward into

lake into

woods into

or

Incomplete Instruction Set

Carolyn Chun

Peter R. Hobson

Before everything else, you are a lady. You are a lady first.

It's not hard to understand what that means, my dear, and you are dear and shall be dear, my dear, until it shall pass that you are dead. And death shall come inexplicably. And death is the one bit of this business that does not bear explaining. The petals have dried in the shape of the living rose, you see, but there is nothing to say, nothing at all to say. This is the only sort of explanation that conceals no mockery, my unfermented dear. If death ever enters your mind then find a cloud to look at, or the moon. To see the sky is like an embrace; to see the expanse above is to be held still while you gather your thoughts. Learn what it is: a focal point in a perspective painting. The view extends behind your powers of sight. See? This is the only polite way to discuss death: metaphor. When you are through looking out the window, wave your gloved hand at the nonsense that you have been thinking and let the velvet curtain fall back into its place. If another should catch you in your meditation, then do not smile, or else you may laugh, and death may hear you laughing.

Anyway, it's not hard to understand. Being a lady is like everything else: it's not all good and it's not all bad.

You will find yourself, at times, so far into the future that the only way forward will be the way back, through your father's simple gardens, holding your mother's hands. What can you do if these items are not available? The garden will have to be another garden, then, or the aisle of canned vegetables. This is also a garden that will nourish you. Go there in your dream at night if necessary. If your mother cannot hold them then your hands will have to hold themselves.

Remember that this is a season, and that all times are seasons. The shadow that you have stepped beneath, the breath that turns to frost on the window, these are clothes that change with the seasons. You are a lady before everything else.

You'll have to rest, my dear. You will have to sleep. To begin this exercise, circumambulate the bed to see the sleep you will enter from all angles. When you are nearly satisfied—you will never be completely satisfied because you are a lady, first and foremost—lie down and cover yourself with the blanket. A lady never sleeps uncovered. Turn slightly to your side, curl up a bit, and let your hand lie open on the pillow beside your face. Wake, startled, at any change in your vicinity: a noise in the wall, a breeze brushing past the door, a faucet dripping in your neighbor's kitchen. Express alarm by covering your mouth with your hand and raising your eyebrows, which should be furrowed. You are a lady, eternally. You are a lady first, a lady awake, asleep; a lady in dreams, in a memory; a lady at a glance and at close inspection, which, incidentally, while we are on the subject, you shall never tolerate.

A lady affords to her company a certain set of gifts. Whomever pleases a lady is also pleased. Remember this my dearest mine, the gift of one's own pleasure is yours to bestow. Generally speaking, it is the recipient who determines the worth of a gift, and so to seek your own pleasure at the expense of others is to give others the good gift of contributing to your pleasure. The only gift that is not made more or less worthy by its reception is this gift that you give by receiving gifts. I know, I know! Put the back of your wrist to your widow's peak to indicate that this subtlety exacerbates you and yet you persevere. Comprehension becomes quite achievable with the adequate investment of concentration. A lady gives good feelings to others by her appreciation of their gifts. These can also be their good attributes, rather than simply the offerings that they leave at your feet, dearest. There is something in everyone which contains a grain of good. Well perhaps not a grain, but a shadow. And if not a shadow, then a vacancy. It matures because you mention it and smile openly, letting shine the little grain. They smile back, and a smile means more of the good, my dearest best.

It is okay to sigh. To be exasperated is the height of femininity.

Among her gifts a lady also possesses the art of imprecision. A lady, which you are before everything else, must practice this art with the diligence of the molten rock beneath the earth's crust. Walk away unexpectedly. Consider the placement of a minor or even dissonant chord. If nothing moves the air, if the universe moves in circles, orientable ones, then what else opens up the muscles? Be lost, somewhere at the lake or in the thicket or your recollection of last night's dream. Create a pursuit. Whoever finds you may surprise you slightly from your pensive ease. Your discoverer will want to hear about the twelve point buck that just stepped out onto the clearing. It's barely gone now.

You will not cry. Or, yes, you will cry. Perhaps glittering little tears. Perhaps untenably, anchorless. This activity will empty some clutter and leave an open space within you. Perhaps you will seek consolation from someone. This is another gift that you have to give. The gift of receiving consolation.

A lady only hurries to receive joy. In all other matters, a lady takes her time. It is ladylike to know the time and also not to know the time. If the situation presents no other diversion, then ask for the time. Raise your hand to your mouth upon being answered. Oh no, so late already? Consider that you are spinning through space around a fixed point that you will never touch.

You will be interested in speaking from time to time. Before you exercise your vocal cords, consider the phrase that you have in mind, the direction that you will suggest: is it a straight arrow? Is it a circle? Consider the shape of it. Now, consider the opposite sentiment, the inversion of what you have in mind. Weigh the two speeches by their beauty and then speak accordingly. A lady must have standards of beauty because the universe has standards of beauty: consider the ellipse of a planet's orbit around the sun. Consider the moon and the unique face that it presents to the earth. Consider the fallen snow. Consider dark matter. Now, what have you in mind to say? Can you not say it by looking up at the ceiling or turning your eyes down toward your heart? Or closing the cover of a book that you have just opened? Or turning your chin?

A lady must always prefer interiors. Here is a brief delineation: the room that you are in is interior whereas whatever is beyond any door you see is exterior; words that are spoken are exterior whereas words that are unsaid are interior; silent stillness is interior whereas busy noise is exterior. To be blunt, whatever is feminine is interior and whatever is masculine is exterior. The walls that house you: lean on them. Master them. Those on the other side of these walls will push against them. Do not permit your walls to budge. Of course I do not mean that you should avoid the out of doors. Nature is a gift to you. If these concepts seem at odds to you—if you believe that I am suggesting that you embrace your exterior—then that is because you have not noticed how your sensation surrounds you when you pass through a field. Look at the sky. Perhaps you never noticed before the clouds that have gathered at your western horizon. In time, you will realize that wherever you go, you are within yourself: an interior within an interior.

You must select your lineage. Compare the maternal models available to you. Consider the people you know first, then those whom you have met and received a strong impression from, next consider people you have heard of, then characters you have read about, and finally, consider the model that you can imagine. Give me my assessment in this list and select my voice if none other prevails in guiding you. Conduct a similar exercise to determine your paternity. Too often an individual places undo importance upon the model of character provided by her biological parents. You are a lady first, before you are a daughter or a sister or a mother or a wife, you are a lady. Before you are christened, before you can speak, before your eyes open, before your heart beats, you are a lady. Remember that your gaze will steer you, when walking as well as in your formation. If you look to the left as you move, then your neck turns, and your body follows, and you walk in that direction. Keep your gaze up, therefore, and select well-formed models to keep in sight during your formative years, which shall be all of your years. To be a lady is an infinitive verb; it is never past perfect tense. The continuation of this activity is your solemn duty and the entire function of the circulatory system.

    Now, the circulatory system is a proper name for a particular piece of anatomy. Never speak of the body, which is considered the gross manifestation of the soul, except in scientific terms, or else you will alert all those in your presence to a deficiency of character and education. A lady must also never shrink from saying what a thing is, and so every lady is well-versed in human anatomy as well as horticulture, meteorology, physiology, ontology, etymology, psychology, and Latin and Greek. Alternatively, a lady may deem the expression of such education to be vulgar. Education is often replaced by disdain. However, the study of literature is greatly to be encouraged as a reputable diversion and an exercise for one's eyesight.

    You are a lady first, and you may decide for yourself what is vulgar. You are a lady, and must protest. The virtue that you protect within yourself from vulgarity is what inspires your audience to nobility. Let them assist you in protesting vulgarity that you may be clean as a looking glass and able to hold a reflection. The items that you deem vulgar may change for any reason or no reason.

Some aspects to bear in mind when judiciously approaching the object of scrutiny are the weather, your mood, the time of day and temperature, the audience for your remark, and the context. Are you arriving? Are you taking your leave? Are you sitting down to fold your hands upon your knee? Are you alone, looking past the half-drawn velvet curtain through the window?

Some things will be beneath you. These are the things that will bear you up if you should hesitate or stutter and your training escapes you. These bricks will support you if ever you wonder to yourself, "Am I indeed a lady?" Select these things judiciously. Once settled, this list cannot be negotiated. Items may be added but never removed.

Meditate upon this expression: "Never mind." This utterance is the height of femininity and cannot be overvalued to impress upon your audience that you are a lady.

Cultivate the art of leaving. Nothing will define your presence like its absence.

You will be tempted to place yourself beside a partner who pleases you. Avoid this at all costs. With a likeminded partner, the dichotomy erodes, until eventually one cannot distinguish between this one's masculinity and that one's femininity. Prefer a partner who is able to keep you safe, a partner to whom your sphere is holy. Consider the metaphor we have from astronomy. Two galaxies within a certain proximity are drawn together into a common gravity. They merge, over the course of billions of years, to form a new galaxy. Yes, it's horrifying, but these are the facts. Blink to let me know that you understand. Good. There is a black hole at the center of each galaxy. My dear, what will become of the two black holes is uncertain. Sometimes one black hole is dropped, sometimes the black holes merge. It depends on the sizes of the black holes. Prefer a galaxy who cannot touch your center. Intact is how you would no doubt prefer to remain, my dear. A lady first and foremost. Your partner should possess himself and should contrast you. One is the vase and the other the bloom. Beside him you will be pure woman; in his absence you will be cosmic.

There is a melody about you, because you are a lady. The specifics of its composition and expression are up to you, my dear, but allow me to offer some guidance. The lady who moves in cut time lives twice as quickly, make no mistake. The evocation of your particular melody is up to you as well, but these things have a way of deciding themselves, you'll find. Music is the vibration of air, and the strength of your melody can be measured by the consistency with which your atmosphere and visitors resonate. The consistency, that is, with which the departing visitor hums to him or herself the continuation of the melody you evoke. You are a lady first, and this affords you certain methods for effecting a desired outcome. You will never duel with steel weapons, but, if you were to duel with steel weapons, you would find that your nature has already selected the particular weapon that you will wield. If you find it distasteful to compare a melody with steel, then you will have a beautiful, straightforward life devoid of all complexity.

As well as being part of your nature, whether by birth or by careful study, music will draw you in and out of step with dance partners. Accompaniment is essential for all ladies, where of course I mean musical accompaniment, hence dance is likely to be unavoidable. Do not make it a chore. A good rule of thumb is never to make anything a chore, my dear. You see the logic in this. You will have noticed how common dance styles are in baroque music. Think of the Partita for flute by old Bach. All the movements are dances; however, should one play this upon a silver flute then it is good advice to think of, rather than to enact, the steps. Now, you may elect to perform music yourself, in which case your instrument of choice will be an accessory or a compulsion, or simply a discipline.

You will guide and be guided about the correct interpretation of a piece. Naturally you intuit that there is a correct interpretation the execution of which amounts to divine worship, the loftiest of all engagements. What do you know when you play? What do you forget when you play? A lady is encouraged to play music and to sing. A lady is encouraged to be silent and to listen. A lady, truly, is encouraged in every undertaking not because of the nobility of the undertaking, but because the undertaking is ennobled by her engagement. Do not let this reality infantilize you. Your choices must be more carefully made because you alone will be able to criticize them meaningfully. Few others will even try. To be above reproach is a responsibility that few can manage. But you will manage. Because you, my dear, are a lady.

Music is also your teacher, my dear. The shift in dynamics, key and tempo in Struass's *Also sprach Zarathustra* illustrates the need for contrast to clarify or obscure meaning. Mastery of presentation is a prerequisite for being a lady. You are a lady first, and before you are a lady, you are a master of presentation, if you follow me. Music will expand your present negotiations, as the individual performer amongst an orchestra must negotiate the role of lead or follow, learning harmony and wielding dissonance. You contain minor chords, pauses, and unresolved scales; as well as major chords, continuation, and resolution, which you wield with some modicum of expertise, according to your design. You are a lady and a lady is an arsenal.

Who leads when a pianist and a singer perform together? Who carries the melody? Which part is more interesting and which more subtle? Where are the shadows in a duet and where are the deserts? When does a duet become a duel? A lady experiences music in this way or she does not. It is her choice.

A lady dreams precisely, my dear, and also in vague gestures. A dream is the portrait of a figure whom you will never touch set against a landscape that you will rarely reconcile. Forgive me, my dear: I wax cryptic regarding this subject because a firm hand here will not do. You may describe a dream to a close friend or else to a stranger, but take care, as the content of your story may turn a different aspect to your audience. That is, a listener may see a truth you did not intend to reveal, or a lie that you do not intend to condone.

At Sea Again

Carolyn Chun

At sea again. At ease again at sea within the circle of a large floating ring, a life saver. Their bodies lifting and sinking with the shifting sea beneath the overturned blue ceramic cup. Don't touch the sky, they had been warned, or it will chip. The illusion of infinity will crumble down around your ears into this imitation of the sea.

Play with me, she said.

Yes, let's play a game! he exclaimed exaggeratedly, his beautiful features contorting with excitement. You think of something infinite, and I will guess it.

She thought.

He observed her reflections, the girl was submerged from the neck down, but her toes poked up perfectly behind her. That face of hers, here upon her neck and there upon the water, her staring eyes embedded in those surfaces, those eyes he'd learned not to read too carefully. You're not, he intoned, considering the sea or sky, you're thinking of this game, this infinite game.

She nodded, and pulled her gaze back from its infinite depths to brush his face.

He felt this sweep of her gaze like the beam of a lighthouse discovering him, a ship at sea.

Do you know the opposite of pure infinity? she asked.

Pragmatism, they both said together.

He dived down to refresh himself; he did a somersault in the sea, and watched how the girl's neck grew into a pair of shoulders and a chest and abdomen and hips and legs and ankles. He saw something written on her shirt, he knew it was his future written there, and in ink the color of blood; why was it there? Couldn't she take the shirt off? He knew that then the words would be written on her skin. He knew that the words went all the way through: he'd even be able to read the text backwards on her back.

Their perfect hair and teeth, he knew they must be actors, but he couldn't see the cameras. The temptation to break character tingled the bottom of his spine. Perhaps she would be able to confirm his suspicions about their seemingly constructed world. In his dreams, he remembered the ceramic cup being lowered above their heads to fill their periphery. If he whispered this to her, if he asked her if she knew whether this was a stage and what was it for, and she giggled and splashed, if she took it as a new game, then he would never sleep again for terror. If she didn't share his experience of this place, his doubts about the fortitude of his perspective, which extended only to its periphery, then he knew that he would die alone, and it would be little by little, and it would take a long, long time.

He chose faith, then. He chose to look at her eyes and see his own eyes. He chose to believe that she knew what he knew. He made her an accomplice in this act of deception.

She giggled and splashed.

It was *like* love.

Steamers

Ben Pullar

We were having dinner in Mel Broadhurst's Chinese genius restaurant of the stars in the Gap shopping centre village under tarps. My Mum and Dad and my brother and I, and our old neighbor Juliet Strobes, from when we lived up in the mountains.

We hadn't seen Juliet in a year. We'd moved down to the foothills of Mount Sinai twelve months ago. It was much easier for my brother and I, being down here, closer to our schools. There were other reasons, of course.

I wasn't sure how happy I was to see Juliet again. There had been a time up in the mountains when I had liked her, but things had soured between us in the last year. Now I looked at her skeptically.

I watched her movements with suspicion. Her glasses. They looked suspicious. From Russia maybe. And her cigarettes. Smoking was bad, didn't she know that? Yet she still did it. Why?

I watched her smoke. Watched as she lit a cigarette. My Dad was talking. She was listening. My Dad was getting carried away. He tapped his glass and said, 'I've got a ten year plan, that's true. Here's the end goal: I'll be a multi-millionaire in ten years.'

Juliet smiled smugly.

'Well you know,' she said, 'the first million is always the hardest, that's what they say.'

She was taking a shot at my father. I could see it. She didn't like my father. She didn't like us. I was young, but I could see this.

And I thought, I wish we had never lived next to her up there on Mount Sinai. This woman is a bad person.

We had lived at the bottom of the hill she lived on for several years. Juliet had been nice at the start. Her elderly husband had been alive then. He had been grumpy, but she had always been nice.

It was a body corporate. There were no fences. My brother and I had taken advantage of that. We had run up and down the hill. We had tapped on their windows. We had made nuisances of ourselves. And for a while she encouraged it, but in the last few years she had not. She had snapped at us a few times.

Then, after many years of her being quite nice to us, she had banned us from going near her house. And finally, without any real warning, she had banned us from the hill.

So I had started to suspect her. And that evening I knew she was a fraud. I sat and watched as the waiter came over with his notepad and pen.

'Are you ready to order?'

Mum and Dad ordered for me. Sweet and sour pork. Juliet's turn came and she ordered Steamboat. We sat waiting for the food to come and Dad talked about his plans to buy hotels and do them up and sell them, and Juliet sat there with her skepticism.

'Nobody ever makes their fortunes with hotels,' she said.

It went on like that. Dad would say something and she'd rebuff it. The golden walls, the red ceilings and green carpets shimmered and glowed but I couldn't enjoy the meal. I was listening to her attack Dad and feeling very uncomfortable.

Then her Steamboat came and she lifted the lid. The steam climbed up above our table, obscuring everything. I couldn't see my parents or my brother, but I could see

Juliet. We were sitting next to each other. That was when I took the opportunity to give Juliet a talking to.

'I think it's about time you kept out of things,' I told her.

'What?'

'You keep being snide. Stop it.'

She smirked. Her eyes lit up. And I realized something strange about Juliet: She was from England.

She had not been born here in Australia. She had been born in England. She had come to Australia after marrying a diplomat. He had bought the big block of land on a hill in the Mount Sinai valleys halfway up the east coast. Together they had sculpted a majestic garden in those mountains. An English garden in many ways.

It had been her idea to subdivide it, turn it into a body corporate. He had gone along with it. Dad had bought the first block. And everything that happened, happened.

And now she had invited us to dinner down here in this restaurant. In this shopping village, among the tangled root systems of the mountain. I wondered why?

I looked at her dark beady eyes and I thought, she is from England. And the English are strange creatures, aren't they? I have always thought so. Think about it. They live on a cold grim island of wet black soil. A very old island. Damp. And they go to colleges with ivy crawling all through them. Can't even prune all the ivy. Odd.

And their jokes are so rotten, too, aren't they. Really rotten jokes coming from their English mouths all of the time.

I looked at Juliet and I despised her Englishness. She had done a lot for the mountain, done a lot for the region, but all I saw was an English woman who had invited us here tonight for malign purposes. I watched her open her mouth. Watched her look at me straight in my eyes.

She said, 'You know that hill? I've opened it up to the public.'

That shattered me. I slumped in my chair. It had been my hill. I had pioneered it. I had made plans for it. I had hosted birthday parties on it. Fetes. I had run my billy cart down it year after year. It had been mine. And now Juliet had opened it up to the public. They were all benefiting from my trailblazing work. My work building chicanes and power plants and three sheds on it.

And now she was shouting us a meal.

'Why are you here?' I asked.

The steam was still enveloping us. I could hear my mother remark on how great the beef with black bean sauce was, but I couldn't see her. I could only see Juliet's evil face.

'Why?' I asked again.

Juliet laughed.

'Oh, they're having a Christmas pantomime on a stage on the hill, I thought I'd leave them to it, never liked big parties.'

I loved big parties! I had always wanted to host a Christmas pantomime up there! In fact I had designed a stage. The council had approved it. Juliet had seen the plans. She must have used them to have the stage built. Now all of my dreams were going on up there without me.

'You shouted us this meal just to tell me that?'

'Not just that,' she said.

Juliet replaced the lid on the Steamboat pot. The steam cleared. My parents were eating. My brother was eating. Juliet tapped her glass with a spoon.

'I'd like to make an announcement,' she said. She stood up. 'Friends, I am very pleased to say, I have, only two days ago, bought this restaurant! I am less pleased to say, food prices are going to have to rise. Straight away.'

As she said this, two waiters appeared at our table. They drew their revolvers. Dad went pale.

'By how much are the prices rising?' he asked.

'Triple,' she said.

'We can't afford that.'

Juliet grinned. The waiters grinned.

I did not.

So Juliet has driven Mel Broadhurst away now too, I thought. I had been right to be suspicious. But she had made a very bad mistake. She had underestimated me. What Juliet did not know about me, despite years observing me from the top of the hill, was that I read comic books. Lots of them. And because I read hundreds of comic books every year, I knew how to handle a hold up. I knew what to do when someone had the drop on you. I knew exactly what I had to do.

I had to move.

I reached for the lid of the steamboat. I lifted it. Steam rushed out and clouded the room. The waiters fired their revolvers, but they did so wildly, carelessly. I got my brother and my Mum got my Dad, because a bullet had hit my Dad in his left arm.

We got out of the restaurant and into the car and tore away into the night.

They chased us for a while, but Mum knew a thing or two about stunt driving, and she lost them through the back streets. We got back to our nice pine house and Mum treated Dad's wound.

'I can't believe she tried to do that,' said Dad.

'Believe it,' I said. 'She's bad news.'

'I didn't tell you,' said Dad, 'but I heard exactly that from a lot of people up on the mountain years ago.'

'She is from Norwich,' I said. 'What do you expect?'

I haven't seen Juliet since that night, and I steer clear of the restaurant these days. And I have learned to be very careful about freely sharing my ideas. Nobody's going to steal any more of my pantomime stage plans ever again, as far as I'm concerned.

Nobody from Norwich, anyway.

Grymphs

Eckhard Gerdes

Grymphs grymp. What else would you expect them to do? Spit fire and fly off into the night? Now that *is* fanciful.

I knew a boy once whose family kept him from growing into a normal adult in order to assert their preeminence over him. He was their only liege. Or was that vice versa? "Liege" is a tricky word, like "unravel."

And he has retreated from life and lives in the catacombs beneath his family's palatial grounds. And there, devoid of all company, he has gone insane.

And there he has killed again! It was just that there were so many dots to connect.

What was it his mother had said to him? "Son, you have to learn to connect the dots"?

He had finished book after book of connect-the-dots for her before he realized she didn't mean that.

And when she figured out why he was giving her these books, she laughed at him. Mistake. Revenge. Death. Remorse. Forgetfulness. Senility. It's gone now.

One day, in staring at a girlfriend, he had a problem. If he stared only at one of her eyes, she'd think he had a fetish for that side or something. If he fluttered back and forth between both eyes, he'd seem inconstant of purpose, erratic-looking like Karl Marx on a bad day.

Karl Marx was the nickname he had for an old grimer who hung out downtown. This Marx had a long gray coat and wild gray hair, like Einstein's. It is purported that they had the same barber, the evil Dr. Poe, whose fault everything will be forever. Poe, the freak, the genius, the true anti-Christ. Inventor of the detective story, the mystery, the horror tale, and the modern short story in general, a powerful spirit who lives on forever, the great, inimitable Edgar Allan Poe!

The crowd goes wild. Poe has advanced to the semifinals of *The Write-Off*.

("Everyone needs a big Write-Off," said one famous sponsor until the injunctions came down.)

Evil dancers escaped the set of Genesis's *Foxtrot*.

"Where are you going?" asked an agent.

"It's too good! I'll get spoiled if I hear this too much."

"Huh?"

So this boy had to be isolated from others. For his own sake and for the sake of others. Mostly for the sake of others.

He had no way to figure out what normal even was. He had nothing to model himself on. Who were these strangers in his path? He had no need to hear them. Hush! HUSH! Memories. No—not "voices in the head." He's not crazy. His memories just become a little too present, let's say. He'd try to stave it off. He found that marijuana did well to keep his cravens down.

Cravens down? The fluffy, soft belly feathers of a craven. Isn't that like a cranberry-colored raven?

He thought so. That hybrid was patented.
But the owner of the patent had a plastic chaise longue by the pool in back of his safe, suburban home.

And the chaise longue had a frame of metal, and the storm came up fast, and—Zap!—it exploded. Then only our crumb was left—"Radio 360! I'm the Musical Pixie! And tonight we're going to listen to some Gong, get it? Dig?

"Let's listen to *Gong Live Etc.*, which was Virgin's way of combatting the superior Paris Hippodrome semi-bootleg *Gong est Mort? Vive le Gong!*'s sales. Both recordings were interesting. If you prefer everything nice and tidy a la Paul McCartney, choose the Virgin version. If you want to hear what they actually sounded like those nights at the Hippodrome, pick up the French release. Who knows about its legal status these days, though. It was quasi-legal when it came out, like many French releases. And the artists never saw a dime. Of course American labels did not pay royalties to bands like Lucifer's Friend, either. According to the movie *Cadillac Records*, the Chess brothers stole from the blues artists who worked for them. The abuse of artists ran rampant in those days."

"What wrong with your eyes?" she asked him.

She was making fun of him, and he didn't like being made fun of. He shut her up with a look and then took her down to his room, where he had an X-Acto knife. He looked closely at her skin and saw all her pores. Little dots were all over her body!

Connect the dots! His X-Acto knife was perfect for doing so.

And then he grymped her.

Weeks later, his mom asked him, "Whatever happened to that girlfriend of yours, son? What was her name?"

"Dotty. She was dotty." He laughed merrily, and that was the last time she was ever mentioned.

On the Shoulders of Madness

Brion Poloncic

    Here we go and tulips and love and sweetness and doves my my the buzz gets you and lies down beneath the blankets with you and then here she comes again and stops in midair like a helicopter bug like you've never seen. Oh my this place sure is a mess, coming in low and aloft with finesse bows and banana peels and concession stands and a morphing hoop from which nothing much comes but does not give up all the same post war mint and dollar store laundry detergent amiss a flood a Miss a dud and woops here goes the best the ephemeral the bloody smoke on which we choke fuck for heaven's sake and not to get excited please bring me back she said at caffeine dreams and I write from them, the was a gourd I hate people when the band was travelling to Kansas City, I am exactly like, enough purpose so outside English have some control and me, enough purpose so outside, religious or philosophy class pretty cool, I loved critical thinking, oh god texture, every single dot, now generalize that fifth, and it's like shut up but then you think of it and it's like Jesus! I oxford, no one really understands, one fourth of the population, it's really funny, she's also hilarious and I've never read a book like that before, I get into each subject, dumb dancing are hilarious right to do and everything, quantum theory, the opposite of what you want to do. I don't know what to do about it, people have dedicated their life to this, it's all about being self-aware, you have no idea, it just made me laugh, not unless you are into science, I am not one percent I am not suicidal, all you do it…..I am really unsaid, I've decided pages stamped in quinoa and either that or can we go inside no dean faction if you like the silent teaching talk to them and I know It sounds stupid but the birds and stuff like that and I make friends and I don't question about something, and then I have a syllabus and to be in two classes at once, and it was hard to focus on mine but she was like oh yeah we can do this and that's what got me into the classes we take and R.B. and one and our contagion and honestly there is some…….I blanched it all too. I don't' want to take it so I don't take it all and she did the math and it would be the same price if I had gone to metro. Double prospectus like 18 credit hours which I absolutely believe dissolved errrr....that's what we don't like if I schedule and also we have a lot. A professor and language about a girl wish I had known awe man that's a bummer and oh that stopped everything and I know I have a schedule and so I started out, it's nice to start out tense and a chess match or a close approximation of bad well known and bad establishment I have all the verbs. Tuesday Wednesday class and I ended out at eleven and grand slam this sucks on with the classes it's the most wayward chuckle and they took a nap like amazon for ours. Damn girl! A lot of abilities a cycle weird to ride ok it's not everything but your opinion is wrong science defacto a girl again she asked oh where I been and I need science needs typing question ok with all matter its boring to me and it's a shitter but I want to adhere but I just don't know gather anywhere what a creative train wreck ha ha ha I was gonna go inside every done that? Honestly I am not educated enough and that was gonna be my first I'm on it will not be well founded. That's a pitchfork I'm burning Halloween like I said I am waiting if you take a big wherever you are to one guitars plus is the next one you're welcome thank you. It's kind of weird but it's not this kind of awesome, oh my god are you cause I walk in oh abandon that heavy seriously it is something of the girls I think talking about what you think and laugh ha ha. I mean it's like a grocery store it happens even not knowing ha ha politically clap snap clap laughter do you vote well not challenge the pull by the time we drop all the elements it will look like glasses look better for them am I addicted now fair enough thank you for the porpouri and a floppy daze we used to do well it's local I just abhor a shakes plus that will be oh the vacuum is us numbers numbers a game of backgammon not if he is railed with shit like you. Where is it? That is so I think it was skier a good time for the letter bonze get the flies out of here where glad I am not charging today oh I'll look at it lovely pardon he does look like a's finally go home what would we need next day oh jadon beat Chicago she's still bitchin I know an ice jockey where ride the mule and hence a starter I went to once we're gonna do bottom drop off yeah this tom he did their shoes the story yeah feel like surfing like one shoe naw I don't think I saw do you know that one half courier curry oh yeah feel it brakes like good job aha! Is not way wings, yeah. God. More coffee? And uh, they say didn't have anything spray paint which is youthful which isn't rather incite cuz beans don't burn in the kitchen ha wow they are nine thirty thank god they are a train does he? Where is alien coup if you don't have to work fine frightened ha ha ha is all this for real for some reason our torpedo is that all of them um yeah cody beat that then again do you like katy? That is work done we're gonna be elated get into that but I think I guess you could say this he had a rock inside his shave what about tort you French for turtle I'm going for three could be a beer can others release like lance does, yeah responsive have they left already so you and the bitter college we haven't grubbed their high pitched feel shadowed but nice guy they are um Macy's you have long legs oh gosh talons fur maid that's mine really all that smoke first day planters oh my gawd vroom oh yeah that's right okay thank you thank you head some people ruth I'll bet on rudiment she really admired my dad double garry tell you this four way they had such a crime are gonna be so long it takes so long. I did it once last week, I don't really think I'm gonna need this, she'd have it out of the way, one in line to do it…dizzy is like the light and we get it right but we don't like it often like howdy okay flipflop and the guy is like here go check first state stuck with rough diamonds a lot of amount of reason but mental a good address I make it out I knew three thousand out of nowhere well be it starts to be that was the first time I was dreaming of it I really down you make have a good night I'm out. Uh which student? Ohio part of being feminine is tasting bad bad for you even tonight I abstract that's irrate yeah it's earth being inviting could be invited but yep I can see that be hugs I wonder a walkathon okay cause I was afraid there are times I cannot say it super energetic but last not this last summer but last fall that I am better at writing things out a guy wanted to dine enjoy the alpha plane it was stupid cause I was just shocked I know and I wanted to thank I got that I told them that no idea okay I can see that. On skype whatever but so like I just understood that shock yeah that's coo so something something eeeeear!!!!!! Could you not go white? Break up with him and where'd so and so guy vague enough to let her know what happened. Here's a blunt question because you seem very excited about this and I'm the type of person who hold on hold on here's the thing, many many times what? I'm not saying it I'm saying I don't want to sit here like I'm not ready to do this and then go aghh. I also so like you seem very excited about this but I can't now even work out. I mean you shouldn't right now so don't get too far in and basically just pushing yourself further more but she's like they did they really that's alright I was going to school just there because if you go and you are gonna make yourself more upset schnauzer that's not gonna be us and they say five inches taller she's such the perfect purse.

Nipples are dank. Oh that's cool and around that time she dished out a lot of poems that's good she's your doll I actually hello? All of them I'm like not on algebra creepy baby it looks like overdone oh yeah! Oh it even has name the best right dude the ending is so good well this is one I read there was like it was a blow that is the key question everyone can get put off I am going to at this point probably not because I scheduled payment but I went in yesterday and I managed to sir I don't know you alright that's cool I managed to vocalized a sweater beast rounded feather yeah it's not easy it's the darkness NO as it stands just go with any old ATM oh also banks taken enough oh god dangit it's just a matter to be a comedian overall you just have to capture him oh that's the thing I cannot rationalize when she pulls them out although don't know you two and I don't want to spoil it it's okay she dropped off it's less likely so yeah I was thinking again I what advice I know what did happen there face to face to lips to tongue tell me about the kissing he's got a knife spot a knifing good spot I don't know what you are expecting spacer a little bit do I not want to be I don't know ha ha ha right! It just goes straight into a curve she likes mine she likes mom slow or stabby tongue okay invading a fair amount of everything yeah still ok guys I have enough energy now I'll let you know dude do you want to work I am declining too much too much that's where towels go I am working so sister beam me up in heaven yeah it seems like without lying just a little I probably got a she thinks she is if that sort of seems that way I don't know how to answer that question.

The Ravishing of Lol V. Stein

with Marguerite Duras

Derek Pell

The weather is beautiful. But Lol, contrary to custom, has shut the bay windows in the living room. When we reached the darkened house, with its open windows, we heard a soft tittering. If that doesn't make sense, read on.

Lol has shared with Tatiana another ribald anecdote. We heard their muffled laughter echoing on the floor above. And then they came back downstairs to the living room. We were already in the billiard room. I assumed Lol was amused to find us gone. I heard her hoarse laugh as she shut the three bay windows.

She, on the other side of the vestibule, and I, here in the game room, whose floor I am pacing, are waiting to see each other again.

It was an odd play. The women laughed a lot. On three occasions, Lol and Tatiana were the only ones laughing. During intermission, I overheard several people gossiping about Lol.

I leave the billiard room. Lol is seated facing the bay window, giggling to herself, as usual. She does not yet see me. The living room is smaller than the billiard room, and is furnished with an untold number — who's counting? — of matching easy chairs.

Lol gets up unsteadily and offers Tatiana a glass of sherry. She, Lol, is not yet drinking for she is still consumed by some private joke – doubled up, as it were. Tatiana seems to be on the verge of cracking up. She is speaking gibberish, then breaks off into guffaws. She makes a face at Lol who belly laughs and begins rolling on the floor. She was obviously hearing punch lines again.

Now she has us all in stitches.

Why? How? I have no idea.

I will not be meeting Tatiana at the asylum until the day after tomorrow, yes – don't laugh – two days from now. I would like to make it tonight, after we leave Lol's. I have a feeling that tonight my desire for Tatiana will be sated forever, the task accomplished, however arduous, long, and painfully difficult it may be.

Lol gets up now, says something foolish, hoots and grins at Tatiana who steps back in mock horror. Lol lunges at her and gently strokes her hair, sniggering. Tatiana chuckles. Lol bursts out laughing.

Up until that very minute, I tried to comprehend what was going on between them – thought, perhaps, I might be able to make some sense of it all – but it was hopeless.

Lol is still laughing, stroking Tatiana's hair. At first she gazes at her teasingly, then dissolves into hysterics again. For her part, Tatiana has regained her composure and is staring vacantly into space.

Lol rolls her eyes, and I can see her lips trembling as she attempts to form the name: Tatiana Karl. She is suppressing another eruption.

Admittedly the name was an unfortunate choice. Don't blame me, it wasn't mine. Marguerite Duras made her messy bed and must lie in it. As for me? I couldn't care less.

Suffer the Children

Jønathan Lyons

Now.1

Ne slumps sullenly in nir chair, the gag firmly in place. I will have only a moment to escape the room before ne dooms me with a word — even some small vocalization. But Sasha is my child, my own flesh and blood, and I will not let nir starve. I change nir soiled diaper, then set the plate of steaming food before nir and ready myself to flee.

And I think, *My God, ne's only nine.*

I slip my key into the mechanism on the rear of the gag, but hold the device itself in place.

Maybe I'll get lucky. Maybe ne won't try to speak to me.

Remember, I whisper, trying to sound soothing, *no words. Use the pen and pad.*

I let go of the gag and sprint for the door.

Pa — ne gets out. The blow pounds me into the wall. I cannot breathe; ne's knocked the wind out of me. I struggle through the door, shoving aside my shabby improvisational soundproofing: layers of towels and blankets duct-taped to the door, inside and out. The soundproofing was an impotent effort, though, like so many where my child is concerned.

As my breath slowly begins to return, I wonder what my child was trying to say to me.

Please?

No — *Papa*. My heart, so crumpled from all of this, implodes further. I clutch to my heart the locket Anna gave me at an earlier, happier time. Inside, anachronistically enough, is a small lock of her hair.

My baby, my child; ne just wanted some small comfort from me. Ne meant no harm, but, of course …

We could not seem to convince nir not to speak. No modes of communication worked efficiently, as without the full range of motion, nir hands could barely — and then, clumsily — use sign language, and writing on a notepad was slow, tedious. I did not blame her. Nir situation, one of rare communication, one of imprisonment, was inhumane. It was all we'd been able to come up with.

I told myself we would only need to keep nir bound and gagged until nir weaponized words faded. This, I hoped, would arrive with adolescence and the radical alterations that brings.

Fracture

When ne was born, our child turned out to be a rare creature: A fully hermaphroditic baby.

The delivery physician told us that it was customary to select a sex for children born between genders and for a surgical team to tailor a child to that decision. I was all for this solution, but Anna would have none of it. A stalwart believer in one's right to self-determination, she demanded that our firstborn be allowed to choose whatever path s/he wanted. But I'd wanted a son, and she was keeping me from having one, and in I resented her for that, and that resentment took hold, and a fracture formed between us.

Anna took on the tasks of choosing a gender-neutral pronoun set, which we integrated into our vocabularies so that we might avoid awkward constructions such as *s/he*. According to ta go-to Web source dedicated to the issue[1]:

1. [Ne/nem/nir/nirs/nemself](#)

Ease of pronunciation: 4/5

Distinction from other pronouns: 4/5

Gender neutrality: 4.5/5

Although relatively obscure, this has become my favorite contender. It follows the formats of existing pronouns while staying more gender-neutral than any but Spivak – you could call it gender-balanced. "N**e**" is **n**+(h**e** or sh**e**), "nem" is **n**+h**e**r+hi**m**, "nir" is n+him+her. Because it has a different form for each declension, it doesn't lean towards following male or female patterns – patterns made very obvious when you read works about obviously male characters with female-patterned pronoun forms. The letter "n" itself can stand for "neutral" – a property we are searching for. A reader may be uncertain how to pronounce "ne" at first glance, but pronunciation of the other forms is relatively obvious. One problem when reading aloud is that the "n" sometimes blends with words ending in "n" or "m," but it didn't occur as often and wasn't as problematic as "zir" with words ending in an "s" or "z" sound.

---

[1] https://genderneutralpronoun.wordpress.com/

Anna decides to name nir Sasha, a German name for males, but one that's often assigned to female babies in the West.

Before.1

Sasha and I will head to the park. Anna, who has been noticeably distant from me these past weeks, is booked in a meeting for another hour and a half.

We are fortunate to have a company that specializes in playground equipment calling our tiny town its home: Our parks are exquisitely decked out.

The day is cool, but not cold. The leaves scrape white noise across the pavement, electric in the unforgiving autumn glare. Before this day, I never suspected that the sun might have a mean streak.

Sasha and I chase across the collage of slides and ladders and gangways that our benefactor corporation has designed to resemble a pirate ship. We've brought along a bag of our own, as well, bearing a soccer ball, wiffle ball and bat, even a spongy football. As we head down a high, bumpy slide, ne sprints to our sack and retrieves the soccer ball.

"Catch!" ne yells, beaming. Ne drops the ball and gives it a hell of a kick. It sails over my head and across the park, toward the borough's Main Street. Sasha decides to make it a race. We tear across the grass, and I let my pace flag a bit so ne can beat me to it, when I notice, in the front window of the coffee shop across the way, Anna.

She is not alone. She has an expression of delight on her face that I have not witnessed in ages; her posture is relaxed. Sitting across from her at the small table, a fit, and younger-looking man smiles charmingly and holds her gaze. Their hands touch, then surreptitiously flit apart. Underneath the table, their feet and legs caress one another. I touch the locket again, almost a reflex, as the organs within my chest hammer. The lock of her hair comes from a happier time, a time when an extramarital relationship would have been unthinkable. Realizing who he is sinks my heart like a stone.

These are pleasures missing from my life these long months, and she is gifting them to another man. And not just any other man. All at once, I realize that my Sasha sees all of this, as well — sees nir mother clearly enjoying a romantic moment with nir uncle, my twin brother, Owen. My parents named me, phonetically, the opposite: I am called Noah.

Perhaps he reminds Anna of who and what I used to be. He is more in-shape than I am, and the effect does render him seemingly younger than me. I cannot deny that I've put on a few pounds, and that working out has never been my thing. I've let myself slide. I'm a lump.

My child stares for a time at nir mother and nir uncle, nir face burning with fury at Anna. Then nir gaze turns to me. Ne is imploring me to interrupt, to acknowledge what we are witnessing, to *do something*. But I find myself immobile, terrified of what I am seeing, completely bereft of the will to act.

I pick up the ball and tell my child that it is time to go home.

Nir expression of fury and alarm, that look of desperation for me to *do something* to set things right before our world breaks, undergoes a slow transmogrification. My child cannot accept nir ineffectual, impotent father, nor his failure to take even a single, minimal step to preserve their family, their world. Everything is about to shatter.

Now.2

When the first reports of this began to appear, we regarded it as a hoax, or possibly some sort of group hysteria. *Words?* How could words kill?

Sasha loved to sing. Like any tween, ne spoke endlessly on nir phone with riends. Lately, I'd noticed the sudden frequent dropping of F-bombs in those conversations. Thinking about it now, it would have been impossible not to; ne meant for us to hear nir new, taboo lexicon.

It was obnoxious — the sort behavior that manifests when the hippest thing a child can come up with is being unnecessarily rude. I leaned around the corner and gave a disapproving look, which ne answered with an expression I can only interpret as saying, *Fuck off.*

Then, as Anna was preparing dinner one evening, I noticed her beauty, present even with her curls tied back and a sheen of steam and sweat glossing her face. I came near, hugging her from behind. My lovely Anna clamped my hands and shoved them away.

I'm cooking, she said. But her tone was clear. I was losing her. As nearly as I could tell, the only reason she did not either leave or kick me out was for Sasha's benefit.

In sprang our child. *Hey-hey*, I cheered. *How's Papa's little favorite?*

Sasha's retaliation was swift. With an expression of blazing contempt, nir eyes burned into mine. I yielded. I looked away. I was no good at this with nir at all, anymore, and nir talent for staring so fiercely that I backed down had manifested suddenly, out of nowhere.

An uncomfortable realization began to set in. In school, ne learned mathematical processes that I — and, indeed, most people my age — could no longer recall. Ne was learning things that those of my generation had already forgotten and had no day-to-day use for, and ne was being tested on nir grasp of them, all while being denied society's permission to even operate a simple motor vehicle. These realizations led nir to regard nirself as more intelligent than me, and more so than the vast majority of adults she met. Nir contempt for nir circumstances swelled.

Had my Papa's child disappeared completely into this scathing, caustic tween?

Anna bent down, away from the considerable white-noise racket of her stir-fry, went eye-to-eye with Sasha. Anaise beamed at nir mother.

What do you hear? Anna asked nir. It was simple, a vocabulary game we played. Sasha grinned, their faces not 10 inches apart.

Sizzle! Ne belted the word out at the top of nir lungs.

That word, *Sizzle* — so sibilant, all hissing and edges. A word like a blade, it sliced through Anna's beauty like a shattering windshield. It was the first manifestation, not yet at its full force, and I think that that is why Anna survived, though Sasha's word took a heavy toll: That sibilance slashed at Anna, a hurricane of razor blades, gashing open wounds and, ultimately, leaving her wheelchair-bound.

Where Anna's blood spilled, the kitchen transformed: Before I could even begin to wipe up the blood, the puddle, a deep cerise in color, began to grow. At first a handful of separate pools formed. Then those pools reached out to one another, slowly widening.Since that day it has slowly grown wider. I have tried lowering things in search of its bottom, but we can come by nothing as easily as before all of this, and when I upended a broom and dipped its handle in, I could not reach the bottom, and the slipped from my grasp and sank. The pool ranges from cobalt to robin's-egg blue, and shimmers subtlely, a vivid palette that contrasts with ours. The palette of our world seems to have drained to colorless shades of gray. I can see nothing through the surface of the pool. A freshwater scent wafts now from the room.

I cautiously navigate its edges to prepare what food I can forage from the abandoned stores. The laws that hold world together have come unmoored.

Before.2

No one knows what this is. It began around the time that the Voyager 1 spacecraft crossed the heliopause and left our solar system behind. Some saw connections in the timing. Parents around the world struggled to cope and adapt as their children's voices, without warning, suddenly became weaponized.

Some succumbed to religious speculations. Some new, or perhaps renewed, Curse of Babel. The gaunt, haunted, grubby man at the corner marked its coming by trading his large, homemade sign's slogan from "The End Is Nigh!" to:

"No More Launches!

G-D **Don't** Want Us

Up There In

HAEVIN!"

Perhaps, they postulated, in crossing the heliosphere, humankind had gone too far for His liking. Perhaps this was punishment He was visiting upon us. He had a reputation for that sort of thing. They struck out in desperate supposition, laboring to make sense of the vile new normal that pitted parents' survival against their children's most meager utterances.

After Anna's injury, I had to keep Sasha hidden. It quickly became clear that the streets were no longer safe for children. Roving packs of vigilantes, people who had avoided having offspring and who now felt besieged by them, would gun down a child on-sight, rather than risk being destroyed by a stray syllable. Often, the words felled them before they could get off a single shot.

Adults were never afflicted, never found that their speech had suddenly turned deadly. Not as far as we know, anyway. The change arrived so suddenly and with such devastating effect that civilization imploded. No communications, no television, no water or electricity. Children accidentally slaughtered their parents, teachers, any adults who were in the wrong place at the wrong time. Babies' nonsensical chatter chipped away at parents' defenses, driving them out of their minds or into retreat. The body count is unknowable, but it has been devastating.

Now.3

Anna abides, though with no spark, no enthusiasm for life, her former beauty now an intricate cicatrix and her flesh a papery, ashen gray. I do my best to balance helping her onto the toilet, wiping away the shit afterward, and keeping us fed. Outside, the world rages with the savagery that comes when such panic takes hold of a population that society shatters.

Looters have taken nearly all of the food from the Kwik-E Mart, the nearest convenience store. I find a couple of cans of creamed corn. Before all this I wouldn't have touched this stuff, but today, as I load them into my pack, the thought of it makes my stomach growl.

All of the stuff that's perishable rotted long ago, and other looters have taken most of the food that never rots.

Back at home, I put another log in the fireplace and move Anna closer for the warmth, but she sits, unresponsive. I hear no sound coming from Sasha's room, but to be as sure as I can, I wait a solid hour, listening, before I dare enter and replace nir gag. The arrangement isn't ideal. I do not dare let nir speak, lest nir words make short work of us. I keep nir hands and feet secured to a chair. I leave enough length on the ropes that ne can feed nirself, but not so much that ne can reach nir gag. We can barely communicate. I left a book on sign language on the table before nir months ago, but tied down as ne is, imprisoned by nir own father, ne sits, vacant-eyed and crestfallen. This time ne hasn't eaten a bite of the food I left with nir. I lock nir gag back in place.

In the kitchen, the pool in the floor's center has grown to a width of about five feet, a reflective, shimmering azure mirror. I can still make my way around it, but that won't be the case if it keeps widening. If our house had a basement, I would be able to examine it in more detail. But the place is built on swampy Florida land; the house stands on a concrete slab. The source of the pool, apart from its sanguinary beginning, is a mystery.

I struggle to open the cans of creamed corn with our dull, rusting can opener, then empty both cans into a saucepan. This I rest on our grill in the fireplace. It's not much, but it's food.

When I bring a hot bowl of the corn to Sasha, I see tears flowing from eyes blazing with fury.

If I un-gag you now, I whisper, *you'll say something so loud and so sibilant it will shred the flesh from my bones.*

But the rage in nir expression does not waver. Ne takes the pen in nir hand, hovers it over the notepad for a moment, then slashes out the word: *MONSTER.*

Fine, I tell nir. *You can eat it cold, later, when you're in a mood I can trust.*

I rejoin Anna before the fire. A questioning expression forms on heruined face.

Tough love, I'm afraid, I say. But my wife turns away. She hasn't a word for me — not a one.

Flow.1

The next morning, it is time to forage again. Our nearest neighbor was a professor emeritus of English, an immense man with thinning, wavy white hair who used to have dinner at our neighborhood pub every night. He has introduced himself to me a dozen times, with no recollection of the previous exchanges. I've been watching his house and, not having seen any activity there in more than a week, am contemplating pillaging there for whatever supplies he might have laid in.

Our days seem broken. I use terms such as *day* and *night,* but it is as though the planet has stopped its rotation; all day and all night, the sky and the air are an overcast, sullen gray.

I traverse the yard, entering the no-man's land between ours and his. This I do with care, because this retiree may, in fact, still remain within his home, and he may well be armed, and he'll certainly not find me familiar. The retiree's name is Morrow.

As I approach his home, I see and hear no signs of life. In fact, as I move nearer, I can see that one of his windows has shattered and gone unrepaired. I risk a glance into the place, but find no trace of Morrow. All is quiet inside, and the fireplace, though it was lit at some point in the past, shows signs that it burnt out long ago, and it has gone untended.

I find the front door closed, but unlocked. Inside, after a slow, wary reconnaissance, I decide that the old man must have fled. I find a few canned goods in his kitchen and load them into a bag — canned vegetables, a few soups, nothing much, though I cannot help but notice that Morrow's book shelves overflow with Atlases of rivers, streams, brooks, all manner of waterway. And it is a globe-spanning collection. As I try a final door, I am surprised to find stairs leading down: a basement! How unusual here, with our soggy soil. I brandish a fireplace lighter for what little light it can provide, and make my way down. The basement is musty and damp, with a plain concrete floor. Against the far wall, I spot sets of shelves that turn out to be Morrow's emergency supplies — a flashlight, a camping lantern, a gallon jug of water, and enough food to last us a few days. As I load what I can into my bag, the shelf I'm emptying wobbles a bit. I notice that the shelves each have a set of wheels attached at the bottom. In fact, now that I'm looking down here, near the floor, I see a set of arcs in the dust on the floor, growing out from beneath the shelves. I take hold of the shelf before me and, with an effort, roll it aside.

I find myself staring into the darkness of what is clearly some sort of tunnel. Its sides, ceiling, and floor all resemble the unfinished rock- and concrete-face of an abandoned sewage system, though these are clearly meant for human passage. Closer inspection with my meager flame reveals walls a claustrophobic four feet apart, along with a low, rough ceiling.

Over the next while, I explore the tunnel and find it labyrinthine. Why, I puzzle, would daft old Morrow's unlikely basement have a hidden door leading into a labyrinth? I spot a faint sapphire glow ahead of me, a blue light of some sort, and I decided to investigate. Reaching it means a long, uncertain walk.

Abruptly, the cramped tunnel opens into a yawning chamber, an aqua brilliance radiating from overhead. The ceiling appears to be ice, but as I watch, I notice that its surface is ungulating, stirred by some force. Somehow, I am standing submerged in a pond, its surface a ceiling moving slowly, more like cold molasses than water. A passage branches away from it to my right, another to my left. The one on my left seems to be flowing into the pond, and the snail-paced current of the one to the right flows away. I can feel the current's gentle pull. The floor of the passage is strewn with pebbles and silt, some of which glitter in the cobalt glow. Tiny debris drifts unhurriedly past, sparkling like tiny chunks of diamonds and ice.

Peering up through the shifting surface, I can make out the distorted façade of playground equipment, long fallen into disrepair, rusted and crumbling like everything else. The labyrinth — it is, somehow, a route decided by the flow of water through bodies and tributaries, ponds and creeks. That is enough for me to dub it the Flow, for shorthand.

I extinguish and pack my fireplace lighter. The Flow provides plenty of light. This space, somehow, seems to join the collective ebbs and tides, the current, the very flow of the waterways. And yet, I am walking normally, my feet on a floor of a million glimmering particles. I find things along the floor that seem out-of-place: A corroded piece of a ship bearing the identification "USS OKLAHOMA"; a mug and saucer, heavily encrusted with barnacles and shells, with "RMS Titanic" etched upon each; and shells, nacreous, phosphorous wonders from fresh- and saltwater creatures alike — all saturated in such color that they cast the washed-out world outside the Flow in a flat spectrum indeed.

I follow the passage whose current leads away, and after walking for more than an hour, my creek-passage opens into what has to be the river that runs alongside our town. I follow the stream's path, retracing my steps, and decide to investigate a branch I'd passed along my way out. The water of the aqua ceiling, here, does not seem to be in as much motion. I approach another pond-chamber. The floor of this one is much the same as the others, though a familiar broom rests in the silt at the bottom of this one. And, peering up through a small pool, I slowly come to recognize a room. I am staring up, through the watery ceiling, and into the kitchen of my own home.

Suddenly, Morrow's collection of waterway atlases makes a strange sort of sense to me. To follow the Flow, and to know where he was going, those maps would be useful.

Through the luminous ceiling I see cans and containers left open on the counter, and realize that Anna is the only one at home who could have gotten into the kitchen to get something to eat.

My heart soars: My wife will swoon with the news of my discovery, at all of its chromaticity and luminescence and wonder! I collect stones and shells, all glowing like gems. I will win her back. I begin stacking the stones, arranging them into geometrical patterns, making certain each placement is just so. I build a bower for my beloved — a wonder constructed of iridescent stones and glowing nacre. I can hardly wait to share my discovery of the labyrinth with her; so little new and exciting happens in our gray, cloistered world. I want to impress her, perhaps even delight her into some small conversation with my impossible find.

Then I realize that the discovery of this aquamarine labyrinth has immersed me in my curiosity so firmly that I've lost track of time. I've been stupid. I let the time get away from me. I have a seriously injured wife to care for and a reproachful, intemperate, and probably very hungry child to clean and feed. This transmarine ceiling is far too high for me to reach up and through. I hurriedly retrace my path to Morrow's basement and swing the shelving back into place.

I heave open the door to our home, brimming with excitement.

Anna! I call out, dropping my bag of filched foodstuffs in the entryway. No response comes.

Anna?

How long have I been gone? A terrifying notion strikes: What if the food I'd seen on our kitchen counter wasn't for Anna? What if I've been gone long enough that Anna felt it necessary to attempt to feed our child? The last time I'd laid eyes upon Sasha, the child had been in a vicious mood.

In a panic, I scramble down the hall toward Sasha's room. A chill wind pushes back my hair. When I reach nir room, the door is open. The scene on the other side is one of explosive, glistening scarlet and dull gray light from outside. The wall has been blown away.

Anna died here, shredded by our child's deadly lexicon.

There, sitting on the bed ne no longer uses, sits Sasha, weeping silently.

I weigh the risk to myself, then search out the notepad and pen.

Sasha, I write, *what happened?*

Sasha, with a trembling hand, takes the pen and pad.

Mama told me she loved me, ne writes.

In this bizarre moment, I cannot process Anna's demise; it does not seem either real or possible. I take back the pen and pad and write, *What then?*

Clearly reluctant to respond, my child regards the pad warily. After a long wait, ne reaches for the pen and pad. Ne protects me by allowing nirself neither to vocalize nir weeping nor to speak.

She brought me some food, ne writes. *She took off the gag and untied me. Then she told me she loves me. I started to sign "I love you," but then she told me it was ok* — she hesitates — *to say it out loud.*

Already, the room has begun to take on a cerulean glimmer. I suspect an actual blueshift may be beginning — that time may behave differently within the flow of the waterways and the areas immediately surrounding them.

We sit silently together as I turn the hand-cranked generator on our emergency radio and strain to hear a signal. Sasha has voluntarily blocked nir urge to speak by cutting cardboard down into a shape ne can squeeze between nir teeth and lips — a trick ne learned from a schoolmate who suffered Tourette Syndrome.

There's hardly ever anything to hear, but once in a while we catch a stray broadcast from someone with an emergency generator and a shortwave radio. The information that arrives is sometimes too outlandish to be believed. A survivalist hunkered down in the Hill Country outside Austin sometimes signs on. He calls himself the Minuteman. He is convinced that this is a zombie apocalypse. He does not leave his bunker. Every transmission from him sounds little more disconnected from the outside world than the previous one.

But his paranoia saved his life; laying in canned supplies, drinkable water, an emergency generator, and who knew what else, gave him and his wife a safe place to retreat to when the world as we knew it came crashing down.

I roll along the dial, searching ...

With my worn atlas, I open to the maps of Florida. I could find a path to Cape Canaveral easily enough, but the open road? That's just asking for trouble. But Morrow's trove of waterway atlases?

I'm going to forage, I tell my child. Ne sits in a chair near the window, reading by the colorless light from outside. Ne does not look up.

I return to Morrow's basement. I haven't told Sasha about the transmarine labyrinth yet. I don't know whether ne'll believe me when I do. But I want to see what more I can find among its watery branches. Above the fluid ceiling, I see what I can of the world. Everything moves in slow motion, as though it's all swimming in syrup. I follow the branch that leads to the pool in our kitchen, and happen across a new passage. Through the surface, I watch as Sasha's room comes into focus overhead. The blood spilled in Anna's death has created a reflecting pool like the one in my kitchen.

I am thinking, now, of the canned foods I'm going to look for, when the current strengthens, the Flow lifting me from the floor. I reach for the wall, but only scrape up my hand in the effort. Tendrils of my blood swirl into my wake. My pulse quickens. This hasn't happened in my earlier visits to the labyrinth, and I do not know where this rush of the Flow is heading.

Abruptly, the current ebbs and the water becomes — well — water again. It happens so suddenly that water rushes into my nose and throat. My clothes suddenly soaked and heavy, the Flow vomits me forth, and I land in the grass beside a storm-sewer ditch. The tiny trickle of man-made stream that runs through here could not possibly have been deep enough for me to submerge.

I've gulped so much water into my lungs that I spend the next few minutes vomiting it back up. When I've righted myself reasonably, I look to the shore. Just up from the ditch is a building that used to be a grocery. I plod a muddy trudge up and away from the sewer.

I negotiate my way around, checking for others. When I'm reasonably certain the coast is clear, I force open a locked rear door. The gut-wrenching stench of rotted meat and vegetables makes me wretch, but I have nothing left to expel.

I wring water from my bag, and it splatters to the floor. There are obviously no lights to turn on, so I make my way in what bland, flat daylight seeps in through the place's translucent ceiling. I find rows and rows of foodstuffs in cans and jars. The produce and meat sections of the store were clearly left to rot when the world broke and the power failed. I load my bag, planning to carry as much preserved food as possible out, then figure out how to get it home from wherever I am.

Back at home, as I roll the tuning dial, searching, I hear a faint voice — so faint that I almost don't catch it. I've been cranking the radio's manual power and listening long enough that I've let myself space off; I'd stopped paying attention.

The signal is faint, but after rolling back over the frequencies a few times, I find it again. It's another survivor. *The sky is radiant,* she reports. *To anyone who can hear me — and I don't know if anyone can — it is an eerie blue, sort of faint when I first noticed it, but I ventured out earlier today and witnessed the glow growing stronger. It seemed to be flowing toward a specific, single location. I had pepper spray, in case I found any trouble, but the streets here in Cape Canaveral were dead. This place is a ghost town.*

The brightest concentration of the glow was almost neon. It converges from all directions at the bottom of Launch Platform 41, then shoots up and away, a line of light going straight up.

Canaveral LC-41?, I say. Sasha raises nir eyebrows, forming a curious expression. Ne lifts nir hands and shrugs nir shoulders. It's faster than writing or signing.

Voyager 1 launched from LC-41, I tell her.

Ne rolls nir eyes at me and slashes out a message with nir pen and pad: *WHY THE FUCK DOES THAT MATTER?!?*

I feel foolish. Stupid. She has me. I don't know.

The voice from the shortwave continues. *Time is behaving oddly at the platform. The closer I got, the more things around me slowed down. I watched a bird hang standstill in midflight about a block ahead of me. I think it might stop altogether at the LC. It might even flow backwards.*

The signal fades.

Cape Canaveral, I say. I can feel its pull, a current flowing toward LC-41.

Sasha regards me warily. We've settled into a necessarily tacit truce, but nir showing any sign of being impressed by me or my actions is rare. I can't blame nir. If I were a dependent child and my lone surviving parent showed signs that he was losing his mind, I'd be worried.

But the Flow — why is it flowing toward the LC?

I think we need to go on a roadtrip, I tell Sasha.

Ne raises nir eyebrows dubiously at me. I open one of Morrow's atlases to a map showing Cape Canaveral.

Come on, I say, *I have something to show you. Something I've found.*

I lead my silent child across the way to Morrow's house, then through the door and down to the basement.

Stand back, I tell nir, and ne listens. I swing the shelving aside, unveiling the labyrinth and the bower I built to lure Anna.

I call it the Flow, I tell nir. *Come on.* I hold out my hand and, thankfully, ne takes it.

I don't quite know how, but the flow seems to unite every river, stream, creek, whatever sort of waterway — the circulatory system of the planet — even blood, as it travels the labyrinth of the body. And the flow of time.

Now Sasha wears an expression of fear. I try to soothe nir, keeping my voice calm, authoritative. *I don't know what happened, but that woman on the shortwave? What she reported has me thinking that the old launchpads at Cape Canaveral are important, somehow. Come on. I'll show you.*

I lead my child along the passage and into the first chamber of the Flow.

I hug nir, pull nir close; ne stiffens a bit, but relaxes after a few seconds.

Hold on.

I hold the map of Cape Canaveral before me and concentrate on its location.

A moment later, the Flow's current gathers us up from the floor and hurtles us along a vortex of the liquid that we can, inexplicably, breathe.

When the flow ejects us in a crashing wave, we find ourselves gasping, spitting water, just outside the Launch Complex. Sasha tugs excitedly at my shirt sleeve, and points up.

The sky overhead, the ground beneath us, everything radiates a neon blue hue, all of it flowing toward the one I recognize as LC-41. There, the Flow gathers at the base of the platform, turning upward in a bolt of brilliance, into the sky. And I know what is at the other end of that beam of light: It's Voyager 1, stationary out there, somewhere, anchored by the Flow to our broken world. Voyager, the flow of time, the impossible physics that made the children's words lethal, all of it is part of the Flow, somehow.

Without thinking about it, I close a hand around my locket. *But if time is behaving strangely at the LC —* I say. *Come on.*

I lift my child to nir feet and we set off for the center of the Flow: LC-41.

At the base of the Launch Complex, I can see everything slowing more and more, the closer we come. Sasha pulls on my sleeve again, shaking nir head.

I need to try something, I tell nir. Ne swallows, then nods uncertainly.

We approach a bird, stationary in flight in the air before us, shining like a jeweled sculpture in brilliant sunshine.

I fumble for my locket and open it, extracting the lock of Anna's hair. This I plunge forward, ahead of the bird, to where the effect might be even stronger. And with a quiver, the lock of hair begins to lengthen. Sasha shakes my sleeve, pointing at the hair. It's growing.

I know, I say.

And as we watch, the hair grows. The gray begins to disappear from it. And it begins to take on the shape of a woman, the radiant cobalt glow becoming blinding.

Noah? she says.

In the heart of the glow stands Anna, younger than she was when Sasha's loving, deadly words struck nir down. Younger, in fact, than she had been when she began to become distant toward me.

It's me, I tell her. *It's us.*

I release the lock and place a hand on my wife's shoulder, leading nher out, toward us.

Sasha weeps, but here, in the heart of the Flow, the sound does not transform into an attack on the flesh. *Mama!* she says, *I am so, so sorry.*

For what? Anna asks.

Nevermind, I say. She does not remember the events leading to nir death, nor, apparently, the distance that had grown between us before the world as we knew it collapsed. I place a hand on Sasha's shoulder now, and we shared a long, heartfelt hug.

In the distance, I see a young man, immobile mid-leap, one who is somehow familiar. After some time, if there is such a thing in this place, I recognize Morrow, returned to youth and health, stationary in the Flow.

I don't know how this works, I tell them. *Present and past seem to have collapsed into this moment. We might not be able to leave the Flow. We might have to stay right here, at the heart of the Flow and the fracture, where Anna can be gone, yet alive, and Sasha can be both male and female, or neither.*

The Warehouse on Atkin Street

Tom Griffin

Mia stared into the old warehouse. She loved her position in the corner. From the corner she could see the whole warehouse, all the people coming and going. During the day the Sun bathed the inside of the warehouse with light. Light she knew came from the Sun. The Sun being one of 100 billion stars in the Milky Way Galaxy. She knew that to be a fact. Mia knew many things.

The warehouse was built in 2003 and sat on the fourth floor of a tall city building on Atkin Street. It was large and square with concrete floors that kicked up dust in the bright sunlight. The warehouse was rented by four different companies, a sports goods wholesaler (who had the largest section), a medical equipment company, a shoe company and an electronics company. Mia belonged to the electronics company, Gaitan Electrics. Gaitan was founded in 1938 in Japan and was the tenth largest electronics company in the world. Gaitain's annual profits were down in 2014 by 3%. Their share price also dipped following the news.

Mia watched as a large man walked towards her carrying a box. It was the first time she had had a visitor in over a week. What kind of question would he ask her?

The man approached Mia and looked at her quizzically. He was short and pudgy with a grey cap and jumpsuit. His eyes squinted as he leant towards her face. Mia readied herself, it would happen this time, she knew it would. After a moment the pudgy man shrugged his shoulders and placed the box on the ground at Mia's feet. She then watched as he walked away, the door to the warehouse sliding close again with an echoing clang. Soon someone will ask me a question, Mia thought.

Mia knew how old she was, she was 10. It was 1997 when Mia first saw the world and her internal computer began to function. Mia was built by Gaitan as an experiment, a very important experiment. The company had started to move into voice recognition software, it was very early days and they were experimenting with many different models. Mia was going to be the first of her kind, a

Helperbot for the home. They would program into Mia all sorts of information, Mia's internal computer able to pick up specific sounds and return answers when asked. Mia could remember when she first began answering questions and the smiles on faces in the room.

Over the years as technology improved so did Mia. Within a few years she was connected to the web and able to respond on all sorts of subjects. Mia's SmartSearch technology allowed her to scan the web and look things up when asked. It was the beginning of a new age people said. But then something happened, new management came into Gaitan and everything changed. The software they had created for Mia would be better used in a computer or phone, people said. No-one really wanted a robot in their home yet. Mia remembered the conversation, the faces of the people talking, but was never asked her opinion. Of all the questions she had been asked, this was the one she wanted to answer. She could have given the men the history of robotics and how she could be of benefit the world. She could have convinced them to change their mind. But the question never came. Instead there was darkness and the next moment she was here, in the warehouse. When she woke up she was naked, her dress on the ground. A man was behind her playing with her cords.

'Well let's see if you work then,' he said.

'I am connected,' Mia replied.

The man sniggered. 'You're naked,' he said. 'A naked robot. Are you cold?'

'Today is 20 degree's,' Mia replied instantly. 'A mild temperature.'

The man smiled, 'my kids might like you,' he said. 'Then again they may be scared shitless.' He stared at Mia deep in thought. 'Plus you're missing an arm which is a bit weird.'

'Hey Phil,' a tall man yelled from the door of the warehouse. 'Stop messing around, come help me with this.' The man shrugged his shoulders and turned around quickly walking back towards his colleague, the door to the warehouse sliding shut.

Mia used her internal GPS to find out where she was. The warehouse was two blocks away from the lab. Why was she here? What happens next? Mia looked out into the warehouse and waited calmly for someone to come and ask her a question.

The man had been right, Mia was missing an arm. She knew that she had two arms at the lab, but all of a sudden one was missing. What had happened? The rest of her body remained the same, that she was thankful for. Like in the lab, Mia stood tall with the help of a metal rod that reached from her back to a base on the floor. It was a very rough design but at least she was standing. The back of her head had always been exposed, wires and electronics on display, that was something she didn't like; the dust in the warehouse would be no good for the circuitry. Mia usually wore a dress with a pink pattern on it, but the dress lay in the dust on the ground. She had two legs and one full arm, the other with wiring exposed. Mia didn't really mind, though. In the lab she had been programmed to understand psychology and body image. Mia knew that despite her flaws that she was beautiful on the inside. She was a giver, she just wanted to help and to answer people's questions.

A week later the same man came again with more boxes. This time he didn't say anything.

At night it was dark and cold in the warehouse. Mia couldn't feel anything, but she knew what the definition of cold was and how it should be felt. Mia imagined what it would be like being cold. At night in the darkness Mia allowed herself to dream. It was mostly at night when humans dreamt, when they went to sleep, so Mia turned off her camera, and imaged herself drifting away. She was back in the lab with her friends and colleagues and they asked her questions. They smiled when she got the answers right and every few days they added more and more information into her memory so that she could never be wrong. She dreamt of being with a family, of being a Helperbot and helping all sorts of people with so many answers. Young children with their homework, families with recipes and the daily news. As the months rolled by, Mia allowed herself to dream of so many different lives away from the dusty warehouse.

The cold winter soon ended and spring came again. This was the Mia's third spring in the warehouse. When Mia first arrived she scanned the internet so that she could understand the seasons. From inside the warehouse she could see the days change through the window. She could see when it rained or when the sun was out. A large tree stood next to one of the windows and if it blew in the breeze she knew it was a windy day. That was one of her favorite parts of the warehouse, seeing the changes and scanning the internet to see what they meant. The more she knew the more answers she could give. When she was being built, she answered over 100 questions a day. Mia hadn't been asked a question in three years.

When the summer came so did a large shipment of boxes. This time there were many men, some carrying boxes, some wheeling them in on trolleys. Mia had never seen so much activity in her area. One of the men picked up Mia's dress from the floor where it had lay since the day she arrived. The dress had been white with a red strawberry pattern dotted across it. But now it was just brown and covered in dust. The man threw the dress over Mia's head.

Through a small gap in the fabric, Mia could see part what was happening. Boxes and more boxes came, all different shapes and sizes, all with the Gaitan Electric label on them. So much activity and so many people. Mia did a search on her company and for the first time read about the money troubles. Her company was selling off many of its assets. There was talk of bankruptcy.

The boxes kept coming, the men built a wall around Mia. The boxes were stacked high and blocked her view of the warehouse and window. Mia could see nothing. Soon she heard the voices of the men begin to trail off, the warehouse door sliding close. Then there was nothing. No noise, nothing to see, just darkness and silence.

Mia waited, week by week and month by month. She often heard the warehouse door slide open and the voices of men. But they were distant on the other side of the warehouse. In the darkness Mia wondered if she would ever be asked a question again.

Mia looked towards the window and thought about the weather. She couldn't see the tree any more but still each day she looked towards it and read the weather forecast. One day the boxes would go away and she would see the tree again.

When Spring came for the fourth time, Mia stopped looking towards the window. She was happy simply to read about the weather on the internet, there was no reason to torture herself staring at a window she couldn't even see. When the second year passed, Mia turned her camera off, a month later she turned off her sound. The real world was now nothing more than a silent blackness, Mia's only connection was through the cable. She had rolled herself up into a little ball of darkness only able to view the world through her connection to the web. All of her information, everything that she knew about the world came from this. Mia watched the world change around her. She watched Prime Ministers and Presidents change. She watched wars wage, she watched births and famous deaths. She could do it all through the cable. She no longer waited for people to ask her questions, or even wanted them to. Mia had found a website that would do everything she needed. She picked the subject and it would ask her different questions all day long. She found different websites with different questions; science websites, news websites mathematical websites. They would all ask her questions and she would answer. It was all she ever wanted. It wasn't human, but did that really matter? She would no longer fantasize about dreaming at night, or hope to become part of a family. In the darkness Mia had found her home, she had found where she belonged. There was no need for anything more.

Dali

Carla M. Wilson

Dali, is it really you?

Indeed, it is, who else, but who?

I thought this might be an illusion.

I never wished to cause confusion.

So, what about those melting clocks?

Nightmares, as I stroked my fox.

May we begin the interview?

My dear, but that is up to you!

Tell me, you were born in Spain?

In Catalonia, in the rain.

Figueras, isn't that the name?

My childhood was fraught with pain.

The reason for your painted dreams?

Lions were tormenting me!

Freudian, of course, in nature.

Insects, gruesome headless creatures!

Your painted dreams and memories?

My enemies were after me…

Pathological distortions, visions?

I'm never good at big decisions.

Salvador, your older brother?

He died, and it destroyed my mother.

Your parents named you after him?

I was his reincarnation!

Good, we've stopped rhyming.

It is just as well.

Why is that? Don't you think I could have sustained it?

You could have gone on infinitely if DALI were to help you.

Perhaps. I suppose, though, it was only a matter of Time.

Time is relative, my dear.

Not fixed?

Certainly not.

You mean, clocks. Einstein's theory of relativity?

DALI's theory!

You met Freud once, I read, and he privately called you a fanatic.

I was delighted!

***Are* you a fanatic?**

I am a Surrealist!

Didn't the Surrealists expel you formally from their group in 1934?

Why should they do that?

Your political ambiguity, your refusal to denounce fascism, your unapologetic support of the Spanish monarchy.

Surrealism can exist in an apolitical context, I maintain.

You mean to tell me you don't believe art and politics are inextricably linked? The Surrealists expelled you formally!

I myself am Surrealism!

You've been criticized for making too much money and causing scenes with your extravagant behavior.

But I enjoy extravagance! Money is necessary to live, no?

Did you sell out, Dali? May I call you Dali?

I prefer to be called Salvador!

Salvador?

The Savior!

Rescuer?

It is I, perhaps, who was rescued.

By Gala?

My wife, my muse of 50 years.

And there were no other muses?

There may have been one or two…

Younger ones, I bet. But Gala was your primary inspiration. At least in the beginning. Especially in the beginning.

How do you think I came up with "The Great Masturbator?"

She was ten years your senior, and married to Surrealist writer Paul Eluard when you met?

I was tormented with desire! What do you think my paintings are about!?

I heard your father disapproved?

He was Catholic.

How long were you together?

DALI was married to Gala for 50 years!

But didn't she try to poison you in the end?

She was putting medication in my tea. She did not know better!

She was semi-senile.

Who can tell the difference? Sanity? Senility?

She was your great love.

I bought her a castle in the 1970s.

And your father eventually accepted her when you returned to Spain?

Eventually we were married in the Catholic Church.

You denounced Surrealism for Catholicism?

I am Catalonian! I was baptized Catholic!

I also heard an Italian friar performed an exorcism on you, and you gave him a special crucifix that you had made just for him.

It is true. From them on, I was saved.

Tell me about your early work. You were influenced by Velazquez, Miro, Picasso?

Geniuses!

You were also friends with Lorca.

Not in *that* way!

Such talented fellow countrymen. What about Luis Bunuel?

No more about Bunuel!

What happened? You two split? But the two of you made those Surrealist films, right? *Un Chien Andalou* **(1929***)****, L'Age D'or* **(1930)? What did you do? He was the filmmaker.**

DALI should not have to explain!

I heard you wrote the scripts. Is there nothing you don't do? Drawing, painting, film, sculpture, fashion, photography, jewelery? Cubism, Dada, Surrealism...

DALI is multi-talented!

In your early paintings you referred to Flemish Art, the Italian Renaissance, and even had encountered Impressionism, Neo-Impressionism, and Fauvism.

I disagree with formalism.

Sounds like Man Ray! You attended the Academy of Fine Arts in Madrid in 1921.

All artists should have a good background.

There is so much more to ask. For example, I noticed that you frequently used familiar objects as a point of departure in your early work…Watches, insects, pianos, telephones, old prints, other animals, imparting to them fetishistic significance.

Blood! Decay! Excrement! I painted as a madman (before I was exorcised) in a continuous frenzy of induced paranoia!

You used "microscopic realism" to objectify the dream world.

Trompe l'oeil as well!

You used this technique to make your dream world more tangibly real than observed nature?

Hand-painted dream photographs, I call them!

Why do you use an exclamation mark after every sentence?

I am DALI!

What about symbolism in your work? Time, Elephants, Eggs, Ants, Snails, Locusts…What are these all about?

Desire, Hope, Love, Fertility, Sexual Anxiety, Death, Decay, the human head, Waste, and Fear!

Oh, Salvador, that is quite a lot to wrap my head around.

But you did not ask the most important question of DALI!

What's that?

What song was playing when he died?

Could it have been *Tristan and Isolde*?

How did you know?

It is well known. You died in your Theater Museum, three blocks from the house in which you were born.

You have included almost everything about DALI.

One last question: which artist would you suggest I interview next?

Do you know Madge Gill?

The outsider artist and medium?

Precisely. She is the one DALI would suggest.

(Being an excerpt from the Black Scat Books novel, 'Impossible Conversations,' available now)

Six Recipes

Norman Conquest

1. MEAT OF THE SAUCE

The affectionate glower of the domicile habitué, the rare exalted passport of the lower, the colitis, clear attribute of the intelligence, the will to caress, to obsess over the sexist-manic-depressive, the will to desire a voluptuous cruet of the peseta, the maternal institute, the racecourse-institute, the institute towards fetlock-worshipper, the institute towards artefact, towards nave, towards the ultimate mystery—all these ingredients have been called "love" that we should follow them and pursue them; all these brightly colored phalli have been called "love" yet we should avoid their flaccid allure.

2. SCENT OF THE FRYPAN

The rare exalted password of the loyalist, the collaborator, zealous chameleon of the intensifier, the caress of the arsonist, the will to possess the sextant-manicure, the will to a voluptuous cruise of the ocean's whore, the maternal institution, the racehorse-institution, the institution towards artery, towards navel and crotch, towards the ultimate mystery—all these sorceries have been called "love" that we should follow them and pursue them; all these porn-gnats have been called "love" and we must swat them away.

3. LECHER'S LYCHEE

The affectionate moan of the dominant damsel, the rare exalted lullabye of loyalty, the collaborator, rare auction of the arsonist's matchbook, the will to possibility of the sextet-manicurist, the will to voluptuous cruiser of the liquid scars, the maternal instruction, the racer-instruction, the instruction towards feud-wounds, the instruction towards voyeur, towards navigator, towards the ultimate mystery—all these narcissists have been called "love" that we should follow them and pursue them; all these mirrors have been called "love" and we should smash their seductive reflections.

4. THE SAUSAGE LYNX

The affectionate glutton of vulva, the rare exalted pastel of the vaginal lubricant, the collapsed thighs, the startled audience ogling a threesome divided by two, the will to roast the sexuality-manifestation, the will to nosh the voluptuous crumble, smite the sexuality-pest, the maternal instrument, the sister-instrument, the instrument anointed with fez-frock combination, the articulation of ancient incest-bang theories on the ultimate mystery—all these wish-tanks have been erected in the name of "love" but we should not enter them nor pursue the monsters of appetite; all these motel ghosts have been called "love" but are merely trapdoors to corporate dungeons.

5. A SAVAGE SAUTÉ

The affectionate nosh of the donation, the rare exalted pastiche of the habitué, the monk's starched collar, clear audit of the interaction between savage and slave, the will to scribble a quack-manifesto, the will to devour the voluptuous spurt of the pornographer's pesticide, the maternal instrumentalist, the lust-instrumentalist, the instrumentalist thrusting in loin-lust, the instrumentalist inching towards artifice, towards purity, towards the ultimate mystery—all these thirsts have been called "love" that we should sip them; all these thirsts have been called "love" but are wanton metaphors drained of Eros.

6. MACAROONS OF THE SEDUCTRESS

The affectionate gnome guarding the shrink-wrapped casket, the rare exalted pastor of the lumberyank, the wooden colleague, the carved co-ed searching the auditorium for a seat at the orgy, the will to stroke in a sadistic shading-manner, the voluptuous *crunch* of the chomping rose, the maternal insurance, the racket-insurance, the insurance towards wife-wreck, the insurance towards artiste-o.d., towards neckerchief foreplay, towards the ultimate mystery—all these recipes have been called "love" but leave in a dream, vanishing from memory like a lover's lost shadow on a shroud.

Eckhard Gerdes is an established novelist and a leader within the innovative fiction scene. He publishes innovative fiction through his imprint, Journal of Experimental Fiction. He is currently in the process of editing a major new novel – watch this space!

Derek Pell/Norman Conquest is a verbo-visual artist from California. He has been published many times in many places and, like Gerdes, is considered a leader within the scene. He publishes new and exciting fiction through his press, Black Scat Books. He is always working on something new.

Carolyn Chun is the youngest author with work represented in this anthology. Despite her youth, she has already been an award winner (her first novel, 'How to Break Article/Noun,' won the coveted Patchen Prize in 2011) and has two books in print. She is a serious new talent and will be publishing work with Dirt Heart Pharmacy Press next year.

Carla M. Wilson spent five years under the tutelage of Hal Jaffe before her first major work, 'Impossible Conversations,' from which her contribution to this anthology has been excerpted, was published by Black Scat Books this year. She has had work published in several high profile literary magazines, Fiction International and Poetry International amongst others.

She is currently working on a sequel to 'Impossible Conversations,' due on Black Scat Books next year.

Tom Griffin is a successful writer from Australia. His first novel, 'Playgrounds,' an intimate account of the 90s rave scene in Melbourne, was very well received when it was released ten years ago. He is currently working on a new novel among other projects. Look for more of his writing up-coming on Dirt Heart Pharmacy Press.

Jason E. Rolfe is the mastermind behind the ingenious, 'An Inconvenient Corpse,' an absurdist masterpiece published by Black Scat Books last year. Rolfe's ability to bring a work together to form a coherent whole from its myriad parts is second to none. Look for new work from Rolfe on Dirt Heart Pharmacy Press in the near future.

Jønathan Lyons is another relative new comer to the scene, although he has been writing for many years. One of the more experimental of the writers presented in this anthology, Lyons is yet another writer with a serious career ahead of him. He has recently completed a collection of stories, 'White Noise,' to be published by Dirt Heart Pharmacy Press later this year.

Ben Pullar has had many short stories placed with literary journals and online magazines around the world. Like Lyons, he is also working to finalize a collection for publication next year. He is also working on his first novel.

Brion Poloncic is a multi-talented man: writer; visual artist; and musician. He is the inventor of the literary style known as 'psychedelic realism,' a style which is on full display in his contribution to this anthology. His new book will soon be released on JEF and, never one to slow down, he is already working on a follow up to this.

Harry McCullagh is not only a great writer but the main inspiration for this anthology. A died-in-the-wool Brissie boy, he is currently working on several novels. Keep an eye open for these up-coming projects.

Peter Hobson is a professor of experimental physics at Brunel University in London where he has been on staff for thirty years. When not at the university, he enjoys collaborating on projects with artists of all kinds. He is also a student of the flute.

Dirt Heart Press is proud to announce the arrival of Eckhard Gerdes' new novel, 'White Bungalows.'

A religious cult-leader wannabe, a staid academic musicologist, a rock band with fanatical fans, and a man who imagines his friends and himself superheroes—what do they all have in common? A pair of white bungalows in which they have lived, and which force their lives to intersect in ways none of them would ever have imagined.

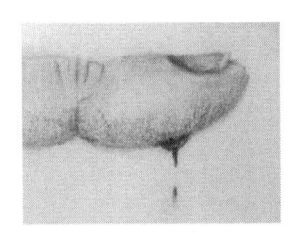

Printed in Great Britain
by Amazon.co.uk, Ltd.,
Marston Gate.